Well-Kept Ruins

HÉLÈNE CIXOUS

Translated by Beverley Bie Brahic

Seagull
BOOKS

LONDON NEW YORK CALCUTTA

www.bibliofrance.in

The work is published with the support of the
Publication Assistance Programmes of the Institut français

Seagull Books, 2022

Original published in French by Éditions Gallimard, Paris as
Ruines bien rangées
© Éditions Gallimard, Paris, 2020

English translation © Beverley Bie Brahic, 2022

ISBN 978 1 80309 059 7

British Library Cataloguing-in-Publication Data
A catalogue record for this book is available from the British Library

Typeset by Seagull Books, Calcutta, India
Printed and bound in USA by Integrated Books International

CONTENTS

TO THE CENTRE OF THE CENTRE
OF THE WORLD

—Where are we off to?

The book had already begun, I was running, I was remembering I was forgetting I was seeking: no sooner had I found than I lost, I misplaced, more and more, I was going down the streets, crossing the squares, on my desk dozens of folders, files, jotters, notebooks, piled up, hundreds, without exaggerating, of pages, of years, from one sheet of paper to the next I found myself in 1648, in 9, in 1561, in 1942, in 2020, two thousand years before me hence also two thousand years after me, now right in the middle of Troy's ramparts jotting down Priam's conversation, Priam the divine elder who looks just like my friend Marcel Dulas, or is it the curly haired Basque fellow who looks like Priam, talking to that wretched woman whose namesake I am not, for Hélène is the name of my Osnabrück great grandmother, Hélène Jonas née Meyer nearly two hundred years ago, from the book's standpoint time is timeless and hourless

and while we crossed Cathedral Square walking faster and faster, as if we were, my mother and I, automobiles that recall being horses back when my mother was the child skipping across the street in front of the Dom in front of the Osnabrück mayor's calèche, I hear, I think, a crowd or several crowds shouting violent words in the transparent air of the very pretty, very calm streets that raced, still empty still shining, this morning down towards the river. Words howling death.

—Where are we going? my mother says, each time that hundred-year-old Ève and I, clinging to each other, shuffle down the corridor that leads from her room to the centre of the house, at her age the passage takes forever, for me it takes half a page. —Where are we off to?

—To the centre of the world, say I. As always.

This photograph of the famous Jonas house at 2 Nikolaiort, Osnabrück, was taken by Lichtenberg, the renowned early-twentieth-century photographer

All Germany knows that no one knows where Osnabrück is. Osnabrück is a fiction. Each time I study a map of Germany, I hunt for it. In the books—so many of them in my study, on my shelves, it's everywhere, in the maps, memoirs, archives, as soon as I find myself there I am lost again, I run across its squares, its streets, its ramparts—I find it, each time new and legendary since Charlemagne baptized it, and even long before that. In my memory I know everyone and all the dates that glow like night lights in the temple of time

So what a surprise, this 12th of February 2019! I don't mean the seventieth anniversary of my father's entry into the other world, which doesn't even cross my mind. It's my first time in Osnabrück Dream! The house (the one in the photo at the Lichtenberg's, Osnabrück's photographer-memorialist since photography's invention) is occupied by the Descendant or the Descendants. Nameless but palpable, obviously. Where are Mama and Omi my grandmother? They've gone out, the Dream says. I accept the situation. I gave away the keys. I've kept one. I need to hide it for my next visit, I think. Where? No letterbox: this century will soon have no letterboxes. A flowerpot? One might forget which flowerpot.

Is it morning or evening?

On the table, a number of documents and several manila envelopes, cello-taped, still sealed. I'm nosy, I want to read the name—of the Descendant—but here he comes. A tall hand-some man, hair surprisingly black (I'd been expecting a white-haired Descendant?). Very white skin, paper white. What astonishes me: the nose, shapely, straight, short, not a Jonas

5

therefore? He was a workman. Now he's a writer; I question him: Since when?—It came to me, he says. I was expecting him to recognize: when he first read me. He says: Almost overnight, a passion. I say: It's always a bit of a shock.

People come and go. As with fictional characters you hear them walking in the staircase, they make themselves at home. Everyone is naked. Not for me, thanks: I'll wrap myself up in a sheet. The Descendant is off to bed. I bestow a kiss on his temple. In profile he might have reminded me of Felix Nussbaum: you can tell he's thinking in images. I discover the bedroom. Midday and it is dark. The curtains are drawn, to darken it, save for one gleam, a pink-shaded nightlight. This is how all the great books begin, in a bedroom, by lamplight. The word 'lamp' pulsates. I use it to peek at his mail, always the enigma of the name.

I leave. The garage, or a sort of barn, the kind you see in the surrounding countryside, open, jam-packed with canvas sacks, triangular, a disquieting sight, backpacks? Bonesacks? The remains? Or preparations for a departure? Is it always open, could one steal?

In the back of the square on the right you can see a flock of female workers, wearing lab coats, they're going away from us, they look a little like ghosts, they disappear down the Hexengang with its narrow gullet, descending in lab coats like nurses? Or like midwives? They're gone

—This is the first time I've met my descendants, I think.

—It's you in reverse, note the nose, says my daughter, a worker in the arts

Let's follow them, let's take the Hexengang. Since I know it already. Down, down quick as a rabbit with Mama. Today as yesterday it seems she leads us.

In the Osnabrück days, my mother wasn't a midwife, in those days this hadn't even crossed her mind. It came later. A passion. An Algerian passion to my way of thinking. In Osnabrück, in 1641, they were still tossing midwives—twenty-seven of them—into the water with their left big toe joined to their right thumb, this body-thing is backpack-shaped, with a head, you let it roll and it rolls into the water, if it sinks she's innocent, if it bobs to the surface, impossible without the devil's help, she's guilty

Midwife says my mother is the world's best job but

There's a place where the Story beginsends, that is, the story of a story, a narrow raised stage from which height you see the future of the past approaching, as the past accumulates in a dense heap at the base of the ramparts.

From this place you see the sum of what is was and will have been *equally* present, equally inaccessible yet distinctly visible. Here, you tremble with emotion. And with regret.

Here you are no more. You are born no more. You know no more. You know, but only with the senses, not by knowing

I remember but it is now, I see us I shadow us, we are happy without knowing it, that's what happiness is, take this day on these narrow streets, savouring the narrowness, which leads—it this a memory?

I remember, is this what you call remembering? Walking briskly, our Stroll takes us past the Dom, we don't go into the cathedral, nor the cloister, now left and left again to the corner where through a window we see the tombs in the pretty garden of roses and tombs—all archbishops—old tombs eternally young garden roses don't count the centuries, peace slumbers here, a little dream in time's strict enclosure, instead we walk a hundred metres further along the square, immense, as usual, an esplanade vast as a ream of white paper champing at the bit for the lines and signs to be set down, we'll come back, let's keep moving along the Hegerstrasse we'll be back, past the Hegertor, at the same brisk pace, as if we're in a rush, Mama, as if she knows where we are going, advances with the firm gait of her sturdy shoes,

I don't know how to say this in German, this is a word for my mother, a word with go and god, something martial, that knows our destination, 'it's as lovely as ever' we think, a sentence that shows our state of mind and in the air, something uplifting, a breath of wind that seems by definition to be part of the City, part of Every City,

Yet we don't expect such beauty in a geographically chilly Hanoverian city historically watered by a few rivers of blood and streams of tears like my mother's genealogy

That it be full of flowers and beautiful up above is a sign, each time this sentence pops up, it is our whole human condition that, with a sigh, we are reminded of, hence this is the same sun that shone on the ramparts in the *Iliad*, Canto 3, of which I speak,

the morning when I arose softly weeping, writes Helen the White of Hand, in a dream in which I watched myself weave a great piece of fabric on which I would depict the battles between the horse people of Troy and the bronze-cuirassed Achaeans, I sensed this was an allegory, not a dream, it would depict reality, everyone was filled with desire for a cruel war, and I too was cruel and full of desire's anguish, as usual, as since each of my childhoods

in my memory of the dream, Helen noted, some people walked over other people while they cried like birds, others advanced in silence, that's all that remains of my dream, the cries and the silence that resounded like the ebbing of a furious sob, that's all, those two opposed sounds

and next thing I see myself climbing to the city ramparts, I find Priam my old father-in-law, waiting for me on the wall beside the Tower, and his old face radiates a strong childlike curiosity, the old gentleman says: Come up here and tell me who that fellow is down there, far, far away, bigger than life, since he seems a good head taller than all the others, and carries himself like an actor, some spectacular thirties show, I'd rather not speak of him, he's Agamemnon, the brother-in-law of the woman I was but this is all so distant now, it is part of another story,

or another dream, 'if ever there was one,' Helen the Troy weaver tells herself and this expression that thinks with such vigour, that makes life and the earth tremble, shakes me like an apocalypse, cries like Act V Scene 5 in the tragedy, this trembling relationship of the past in the present, *if this past was ever true,* such is the pain for which literature prepares a bed and a refuge, if one day, to be sure, that day ever was, this is what I was, the sentence's shadow murmurs, if—(that)—day—ever was,

but the sky, the sky is so lovely, an immortal blue, like the sky on 1 March 1571, the anniversary of the day of his birth, when he was still burning to write the completely naked book of his whole and wholly naked self, Montaigne enters—for the small portion of life that remains to him—the volume of the library-sanctuary dedicated to painting, to remembering and which contains all the books that silently meditate, within his soul he has Rome and Paris and all time,

and from the third floor of his library he overlooks the forest and the extraordinarily clear blue sky,

once he is within himself then he imagines, he conceives in his soul the City become Book placeless stoneless plasterless woodless and completely immortal,

the narrower the room's furniture, the farther and more boundless the soul's vision, and the sky with all its stars covers the ground floor as in a drawing by Kepler, which in no way keeps it from being as blue as midday

Let's get back to our stroll, what a beautiful day it is in Osnabrück, the sky and the blueness of its fabric, we think, as magical as a theatre curtain, all we have to do is contemplate it, rapt as the watchman who embraces all time in the staircase of *Sodom and Gomorrah,* and we are transported, my mother and I, into the generations and archives of our interior and outer towers,

what is strange, I tell my daughter, is that I was born for the first time, of my father, in a city without towers and without a river. From then on I was always born of my mother, with a tower and river from one city to the next

If you can call it a Stroll, our hasty, forgetful walk, which leads us along the Hexengang, ineluctably, towards the Hase, the destination and end of Witches Road. It's so short but it is long. It is charming, we forget about the terror, we feel ourselves alive, violently, the little brick pavers are still as red today as they were five hundred years ago, the play of light and shadow, the sense that the Gang is long is no doubt due to the street's different parts, a tunnel with the feeling of a distant horizon, a bend, another, a section that slopes down between two high walls which, were it longer, would feel oppressive, prisonlike, all the impressive charms of a labyrinth, the modest defile between two serious-looking, imposing buildings to the right of the Dom, to the left of the Carolinum Gymnasium between Church and Empire, only between noon and two o'clock does the sun manage to let a little light into the darkness of the human heart.

Twenty metres further and death. Twenty death steps, the last twenty. Frau Skiper was already in a state of death after her arrest and imprisonment and treatment in the Bucksturm. The tower is now a museum for the cries of the soon-to-be executed. On the average twenty cries per victim, according to Meister Dietrick, executioner, who postulates $133 + 121 + 44 \times 20$ cries, which makes 5960 cries noted over the course of his career, including during the years without torture

Hexengang, the Street of Witches, Osnabrück

If only the Hase could speak like the Scamander, it would bear witness to the outrage and the violence against it, making it swallow bodies of women, whole, such a nauseous little river. But it is reduced to silence, like the corridor-funnel of the little street, like so many abused, soiled places.

I remember, and yet in exterior reality, I never went there with you in flesh and blood, only with your shadow.

—Do you remember Frau Skiper? I say.

My mother: The dressmaker? By '39 she'd already killed herself.

H.: No, the midwife. They dragged her here, feet bound to her wrists already roped to the ladder the better to be thrown in the Hase for the *Wasserprobe*, and when Meister Dietrich the executioner lifted up the ladder she was already dead, everyone saw her. So he said clearly the devil broke her neck, all he did was break the legs, not without sweat and tears, *nicht ohne Mühe und Arbeit*, here was proof. (But according to my mother Frau Skiper had no doubt killed herself, in 1561 what hope did she have? Whereas in '39 Frau Skiper the dressmaker could have joined Frau Engers the modiste in Amsterdam. One does one's best to believe the impossible possible.)

—Do you know *Ilex*? my mother says. No? It brings that poor man to mind. The journalist who dared to be anti-Nazi across the street from us at night he printed his *Petit Clandestin*

Libre. Ilex wasn't his real name, Ilex reminds me of Silex without its S, in the end they kicked and beat him and dragged him barefoot round the city, the rope round his neck, and the crowd howling all the way to the Hase, Omi didn't want me to look, I was visiting for her birthday so this was in April '33 and in order to suggest she leave for Paris with me and Eri, I don't like to be a burden, she said, which was both true and false, she didn't want me to see what I saw, but Baruth followed right to the end and I looked, a brief little chap ringed by a crowd, not a lot of people, all colossuses, the Stormtroopers, passers-by who smiled for the photographer, shopkeepers, poor little Ilex, *Ich bin Ilex* in big gothic letters on the sign they make him carry, very high, no one knew what *Ilex* meant, I went away again and Omi stayed. Ilex, Hitler's opposite, Baruth said from the Synagogue pulpit and that's all. Ilex means the one who was neither Nazi, nor Jew, nor Aryan, just a just man Baruth said and perhaps the last in any case in Osnabrück. Poor little Hase, my mother says. And on 14 October 1935 Herr Pinkus was found dead in his garden, dead of grief, the 14th was my birthday, Herr Pinkus who wrote us poems for our birthdays, do you recall? Did he kill himself, or did sorrow kill him, it's unclear, it's always the same question and the same response, we are killed, the rivers and gardens are filled with sorrow

follow me, my mother says, it's strange how in dreams and on our magic walks she is forever trotting along in front of me despite her one hundred and three years of age, you'd think she was a goat and I tagged along struggling as in an allegory of the 'creation' of a text that outpaces me, I stumble, I think only of the means of transportation car, train and, yesterday, transatlantic, I fear the ship is going to leave without me, only this is not an allegory, and I'm following my mother around her mythological cities, over here is the Schwedengasse, where I attended secondary school in 1925, my mother says, with Toni Cantor, the daughter of the rich poulterer her whole family was killed she is still living in Israel, in 1925 I was thinking a lot about the War, the night before my father went off to his death in his German infantryman's uniform and do you think we knew we were on the cusp between two wars and had my father survived would he have been deported like his friend Philip Nussbaum, a cavalry officer in the first war, to end up the complete opposite in the second?

the times pile up, I turn onto the Schwedengasse

I turn onto the Schwedengasse, it too is narrow, however its name confirms that this is the slender path the Swedish took during the ferocious years when all of Europe ripped into all of Europe, where were they going, weighed down with weapons and in a hurry to eat, the City was devoured raw by its occupants, famine, famine, I arrive at the back of the theatre and slip into the cloister with its little garden of death, where I sit down, as in the silence of another time.

What am I doing here, I wonder. Why have I come to Osnabrück? the Question never tires of asking me, I'm amazed, amazement persists, indefatigable, I unfold the city plan on my lap, and with hungry eyes I devour this schematic summary of a landscape, as if on it I might find the answer, the sort of thing that might happen in an Edgar Allen Poe. Or not.

This is not a 'Return'. I've never wished for a Return. In my opinion there's no Return anywhere, ever. No one will ever return to Osnabrück.

This is archaeology. Its purpose is to unearth the city's hidden force, which draws me irresistibly, the way the orchid attracts the bee with such force that the Proustian narrator draws from it fuel enough to pursue an inquiry into humanity's utmost confines. The City contains multitudes of enchanted places. For ghosts it's a feast. Triumph is in the air. It is a special case. It's as if Tipasa had been measured and rebuilt in every detail, or Pompei or Troy, after the last bombardments destroyed 60 per cent after the city's seven previous destructions. It feeds on demolition. Café Alex: here is where I felt myself shiver with a sort of virtual cannibalism. Café Alex has set its tables in our place, my mother says, everything is instead of everything else in this little city,

one time feeds on another, here's the Jonas family home, and were it not for the famous photographs of No. 2 Nikolaiort still extant in the Lichtenberg Museum, the memorialist-photographer more faithful than any memory bearing witness to the fact that this used to be and still is but differently home to Jonas Cuirs and Peaux, 1882, who could see what I see as I sit with my mother at a parasol-shaded table while she reads the *Speisekarte*, eyes running line by line down the menu's pages exactly as she peruses official documents, not to lose a crumb of this cannibal menu, absorbed in Alex as the whale absorbed Jonah, I note the seductive discourse of Alex, successor to the Jonas Family.

Herzlich Wilkommen

In deinem Osnabrück Alex

No. 1-2 Nikolaiort

Make a reservation for two at your Osnabrück Alex

Today is such a beautiful day

Come and spend your lunch break on your favourite terrace

I await you

Your very own Alex

Noodles in white wine? Home-cooked at your Alex

Located in the heart of Osnabrück

Your Alex is perfect

Your all-in-one Café Bar Bistrorant Alex morning noon afternoon evening all times for all ages all generations, dogs included gastroconcept, highpoint of German gastronomy since and forever

French taste German flair is the Feeling of Your Alex Savoir-Vivre from eight in the morning croissants freedom relaxation hospitality hundfreundlich

Your Alex welcomes dogs

Dozens, a hundred photos of ice-cream, tarts, each and every daily special by the hundreds, this is what we've become I tell my mother, an eatery, not far from the Cave, the Osnabrück

Gestapo-Keller im Schloss, the other stomach, kept in the castle, a narrow, stuffy cell in which up to twenty-five prisoners are locked all day long, packed in until hope's last gleam is snuffed

what do they think, the prisoners, this one, what is he thinking?—yesterday in his big, airy clothing store in the *Grosse Strasse*, today the concept of Big wide high sky air room place is irrelevant, it's the Cage, a raft with walls and no windows

when the *Medusa* ran aground on 2 July 1816, one hundred days to the day before the wreck of my grandfather, Michael Klein, I wonder which of those trapped in the watery hell of the raft first started gnawing on the flesh of the other, in their mind, only in their mind, and when and how does the image of the meal arise? According to Dante, it happens after four days in the cave,

when is it that the instant hope, snuffed out, starts to rot, and despair, a kind of tortured hope, quivers and germinates?

but according to the books of the dead, the throngs of the condemned, the imprisoned, escape the inevitable for they have all become inedible.

The speed with which one is divided from the world of the previous day, just the previous day I was asleep in my bed, we resided, the house existed, dishes, curtains, faience stove, if all that ever truly was, and suddenly my mother says, there's no 'all of a sudden' any more, it's as if—there is no more as if—as if you have as a mirror the Menu of Alex's innumerable delicacies complete with colour photographs absent the many examples compiled by Ovid, you couldn't imagine the speed of the metamorphoses. You change species and you forget changing.

Such is the case of most of my mother's Osnabrück acquaintances, those who were German on Wednesday and on Thursday the world was a Police Station. Everything is yesterday. In the Schwedengasse it is as if we had never existed. Only the cobblestones remain

This is what Eve, my mother, must have felt when an unexpected turn of events brought her back to Osnabrück a long time after the world ended. Not one bit like Ulysses. The Return of the definitively expropriated. There's no word for that. Only a mental specification. And the heart anesthetized.

—I was sipping café liegeois topped with whipped cream, my mother says. As if Jonas Cuirs et Peaux had never been here, here,

The complete opposite to me. I am drawn. I have not been scared away.

This is the enigma: What year was it Eve came to come back to Osnabrück? The debate is heated. H. says: In the 90s. Not long afterwards I wrote *Osnabrück* which was Eve's 1999 secret name. Didi says: Not before, the proof is that that's the year she married Pierre-François my son the mathematician; dame Karin, our expert in dates, says '85. H. says: '94? In '94 I wrote I will never write about my mother. The archivist is mum. Mum doesn't know. H. thinks: I wrote it as soon as Eve came back. Eve's comeback. The secret says: And what if you'd written

Osnabrück long long afterwards? Mum says: H. dates nothing. All these dates are fictional. Then Osnabrück sends Martina Sellmeyer, who led the research in the country and beyond in order to establish once and for all, and right down to you the Violent History of the City, we meet her in a street just as Telemachus meets Athena in the person of Taphos, and she says: '85 or '86. We protest. Karin, our expert in dates, says: On the photo Eve looks so young, P-F says: Eve always looks young, Sellmeyer says: What will the archives of *OZ*, Osnabrück's daily newspaper and fortune teller, say? Wait and see.

The morning is glacial and charming. In Osnabrück paths cross a lot. There's always some long-ago divinity. In front of the hospital, Sellmeyer's handsome face resumes time, she is no longer an archivist, she might never have erected this magnificent pearl-grey-tinted monument that takes up more and more of my interior space, this glossy paper pyramid whose treasures and ashes would require years to sort through

—Peter is dead, she says. At these words my mind mourns Peter Junk. He was an inner friend, closer than a relative, delegated to resurrections and I will never have known him in the flesh.

I have left it almost too late to come, I tell myself.

This is the third first time I've come to this city that is more than a city. This is a city you are always coming to for the first time, I tell myself, and there is no other. It used to be the city-to-which-I-will-never-go. As far as my mother is concerned Osnabrück no longer exists. It's like the Jonas residence at 2 Nikolaiort in whose stead *Dein Alex* does business, never suspecting that it dances on a bombed, utterly effaced tomb. Nonetheless my mother has come back or come to Osnabrück one single time, whereas she did not and will never have returned to Algiers, not even in a dream. What is surprising is that she regularly returned to Barberousse prison in visions, dreams, evocations, hallucinations, as if the prison was not Algiers, she kept her prison, they didn't take that away. As if the prison, Barberousse, that is, was an independent territory, not part of the city's inner workings, a world apart, a mysterious country for the initiated, to which my mother was attached as to her big ring, she kept her prison, they didn't take that away,

Barberousse has something honest about it, my mother thinks, it was a prison that didn't try to hide the fact, whereas Osnabrück hid its carceral nature under its well-kept, even elegant exterior, and it practised this (frightening) duplicity as if it itself had nothing to do with it already in 1927, already the last year of secondary school the venomous remarks flitted around the classroom, and already in 1926 and even before that my friend Toni Cantor's rabbit-fur collar was known to be full of Jewish shite, shite shittier than ordinary shite, right when Omi my grandmother, Aunt Meta and Frau Engers were treating themselves to the mythic tarts at Leysieffer where you were still welcomed with a fawning Circe-like smile

In '27 or '28 you ordered, no sooner had you ordered than you were snared in the net, the noose tightens,

Snap

at that moment my mother is very far from the net, what is striking I tell my son is that Osnabrück is not the place where

Eve was arrested and imprisoned but Algiers, on the other hand, free as the wind

I revolve around Osnabrück as around the Sun, I say this with astonishment, like a confession and a curiosity, I watch myself revolving around its colourful manège

you might say the opposite, my son says, as the Sun around the Earth,

what fascinates me is the mixture of light and shadow

what fascinates me is the mystery of the fascination

such a little city, my mother says, without even a university, one river, some ramparts, medieval towers, cells for prisoners, trees, not even a synagogue until my grandfather got the idea, who'd have thought

—and yet revolve I do, what accounts for this city's force, not a capital not Venice not Rome

and yet it's the centre of the world, the umbilical cord that sets me in action

—the centre around which you turn is wherever you locate your object, it is objective, my son says

the centre, there's my password, the Osnabrück compass point is the secret centre of a vast crowd of ghosts, no sooner do you walk past the city hall than kings, queens, ambassadors, painters, priests, crooks, market gardeners, farmers, dictators, regiments, jurists in their thousands rustle, palpitate on the marketplace between Marienkirche and Saint Peter's Cathedral, my study and my observatory and my goad

I place myself, at the crossroads of Krahnstrasse, Grosse Strasse, Marienstrasse, Schwedenstrass

—neither Paris nor London. One never places oneself in the centre, but in order to believe one understands the world, to paint it so as to construct a book, that is, the life's story, I have to find myself a centre of the world. Without a centre it's all but impossible to create. Things must be connected to a place. When Kepler went through Osnabrück coming back from Amsterdam on his way to Weil der Stadt to see his mother, he didn't stop. In his mind he was turning over the main question: there has to be a *harmonia mundi,* I'm going to find it, and across lands he went, clinging to what was for him the central question.

Take Osnabrück: Osnabrück is the point or panoptic point from which I may observe all the rest. It's a sun or Jerusalem or Rome, scaled down. You take a hill, a tower, a belfry, you climb a ladder and from there you scrutinize, you reflect, you seek the meaning. One April morning you find yourself on the Hospital's top floor on the city heights as on Mount Janiculum, the sun is dazzling. In the distance but perfectly delineated you make out the long chain of Teutoburger Wald whose sublime syllables awaken vaguely epic memories, here-over-there nature and war clashed, I think I recall poems but it is so far off and the distance affects me like a prayer: Remember me?—I'm trying to. My ear strains

So you tell yourself: This place is one of its kind in the world. And I sense that today I pass into the thirties of many centuries, from the first right up to the twentieth, including the eighth, and into more than one historical Tale, from Tacit right up to 2020 and its new archives. Each time someone says: 'This place is the only one of its kind in the world,' it is true and I am moved. To each his own time and his own sacred place

Each one and only place is given to each lucky donor exclusively and by means of a written donation. And the existence of a time proper to each chosen observer is the foundation of the theory of relativity, my son says.

Osnabrück's special charm resides to my mind in its stubbornly resonant name. It's the telephone ringing in my mother's stories during our Oran childhood. Everything began with this ringing. OS NA BRÜCK is the first telephone and the first telephone cord. Whenever this oh how antiquated and familiar telephone rings, I'm transported in a second into the times of time. The secret is in those three syllables.

—Listen!

—I listen! I lift the receiver and my memories are on the line, they crowd in, populous, not just the one keeping the line open, which isn't easy, needless to say, but a throng of borrowed memories grafted onto mine, cutting in, entangling me, I house my mother's memories keep her universe alive, a store of unconscious selves, when I'm asleep they turn up green and hard, most of all I love the compressions of the times of events and surprises, like droplets beading my line, I like being in 1648 in October 2019, it's joyful even when it's frightening, how rich and lively and pulsating with surprises the present is, I tell my son—do you remember the Walhalla? I ask. Is that in Strasbourg? my son says, in Osnabrück, I say, or perhaps in Strasbourg-Osnabrück, a romantic seventeenth-century hotel, perfect for dreams and films, there anything can happen, I say, I'm on the line says my son, when memory unreels the proximities are not temporal, this is what I for my part notice as I enthuse in English to my German host, the lanky Oberbürgermeister of Osnabrück, enjoying our tête-à-tête over lunch in the Walhalla's dimly lit little dining room, a discreet modest elegant room, dated, my mother says, so as to advance my argument, hoping to win the Mayor over to my political views. On the one hand it's a question of absolute equality and freedom for religions, and on the other to surpass them, set them aside, allow them to quietly snooze on earth while we keep on towards the school of the stars, I paint this Voyage of courage to the city's Number One dignitary, we must overcome centuries of opposing views, useless, murderous struggles that, seen from the Moon, look as minuscule and vainly violent as two columns of ants battling over the cadaver of a bee, there are murders, cannibalistic acts, teeth that grind and crush, I sense I am succeeding in conjuring up visions in Herr G.'s eyes, the flashy toys a child plays with in the grandiose ruins of an arena, Roman maybe, neither the Romans I say nor the Germans were Judaeo-Christian and yet they lived and reigned, and all of a sudden, who should walk into the room, you'll never guess, I tell my son, Hitler! Impossible not to recognize him, don't you think?

—There's no way that could have been Hitler, my son says

—It was him, I say.

—They'd never have let him in here. In the Walhalla.

—It was him, I say. Do you believe me?

—If you say so. I believe you, but I don't know what I believe when I believe you

—The room isn't that big. He walked right past us. He snuffled, and I was so surprised I almost yelped

—You here! What are you doing here?! Stupid words I remember having uttered in 1985 to another celebrity when I was having trouble at Checkpoint Charlie. It was as if I doubted the legitimacy of her being there whereas I myself was merely one of many apparitions. And she said—What's it to you? Mind your business! In English, in fact. I still hear the famously beautiful voice hiss like a serpent.

I didn't reply. This was in 1926.

—And how did you hear about it? From Eve?

—It was in a novel by Erich Maria Remarque.

Eve never met him. She liked to walk down Bierstrasse because of its half-timbered houses. But that summer she went camping with Otto Rosenthal in the forest towards the Nette.

—He slept in one of the rooms here, I say. In my bed perhaps.

—I was only ever in the restaurant, my son says.

What do we know about ghosts?

As I am recounting this event, here also means facing Herr G. behind whom Hitler has just walked, and if the tall oak and pine trees that line the Arcachon driveway stand in the Walhalla too, this isn't a problem. My son believes I am able to see Hitler enter the Walhalla's cosy little *Halle*, I noted he was taller than I'd pictured. Initially I feared the ghost would spoil the Walhalla for me, I had indeed let myself imagine that the Walhalla belonged to me, such was my prerogative, here where a life had begun, a night of passion, a book had germinated, the way Strasbourg Cathedral Hotel is mine, we acquired it my beloved and I through an act of passion, first us two, later my mother and I stayed there, despite its being rife with staircases even in the rooms, like Montaigne's tower that we secretly took possession of twenty-five years ago.

On the honest and seemingly attentive face of our high Host I remarked nothing. Did he know this charming and venerable hotel had held Hitler under its roof?

Certainly there are many political, economic and ethical reasons not to shout about being touched by a ghost here, as in hundreds of German places. Later I felt a literary satisfaction, finding myself nose to nose with Hitler in the present of 1926 does not disturb me, it helps strengthen the characters. This moreover was merely a prefiguration, a proto-Hitler, the weasel air, half a third of Hitler, what he'd been since the 1923 Munich beer-hall putsch, it reminded me of the Khmer Rouge when they were in Sihanouk's court an overexcited lot whose arrogance was breath-taking. And as he walked past Monsieur G. he sniffed three times.

According to the archives, tomorrow party officials will be meeting in Weimar, is this why he stopped over in Osnabrück?

H. hears about Hitler being there on 27 May 2018, a Sunday. She wonders if Eve really never mentioned it, since it was in the paper, she didn't read *Vorwarts* because in 1926 she wasn't suspicious, she was sixteen, had a type-cast seductive ego-ist of a first love, but that story would take us all the way to the United Nations

What did the City think? I must ask Karin, my consultant for dates, if there are traces

Only on my third expedition—from innocent visit I've prog-ressed to an increasingly well-mapped campaign, henceforth I go like Champollion, ebullient at just the thought—did I 'see' the Old Synagogue, but not really, I mis-saw it, saw it by accident, I saw without seeing it, I looked past it in a striking instance of the purloined letter, I felt a cloud darken my right eye, I rubbed, in vain, it made things worse, stirred up anguish, smeared it on all my eyes, I find myself in the obsessive state of mind of the twentieth-century archaeologist who thinks he's found the sacred site of the originary scene his teacher the nineteenth-century archaeologist had sought in vain, time passes, I cross and re-cross spaces, I feel the little yellow lesion in my eye suppurate, I cross mountains valleys tides, I grow old, the end of the twenty-first century awaits me, head down I advance defeated in the Rolandstrasse, as if I crept around among the dead in Roncevaux, I think of all my friends abandoned over the years on the side of the road, whose names but not faces are effaced, a thought so sad that at the end of this walk I say, I give up, I'm going to have coffee in the Walhalla, I'm looking and I no longer know what I'm looking for, one of these days I'm going to be eighty-five years old I think, sounding like Stendhal and Derrida, and that's when, suddenly, as my mother in her tales says and Homer in the *Odyssey*, suddenly in front of me or me in front of It! I confess it's greatly changed! I'd need a good chapter to paint it in writing and maybe the writing won't be powerful enough, not the right way to approach it

So I promptly begin a new notebook, a small one, to be precise 14 x 10 cm, 64 pages, graced with the photos of ten predecessors' notebooks; on the last page that she mistook for the first, my mother's handwriting inaugurates it with firm and authoritative strokes thus: 30th August 2007 / departure Arcachon / Paris. We'd left. Then 64 pages without a word. 64 blank pages of departure. Eleven years later I picked it up and everything had changed. So I recall my emotion, it was a lovely month of April, the Osnabrück month. I jotted the quicksilver details down effortlessly like a musician ecstatic at the abundance of light, inspiration kept pace with me, I wrote the notebook's name on the facsimile of Chateaubriand's notebook the one that accompanies *Mémoires de ma vie*, I wrote these words to myself: 'begin with the little BN 18 notebook.' Knowing that I had laid the first stones of the book to come brought me peace and allowed me to patiently traverse a long fallow year. Food for the soul.

My tranquillity abandoned me on 8 May, a brutal day when my little notebook vanished. Gone. We hunted high and low. Gone. Gone. Cruel word. There's a knife in it, a touch of malice, terror, a rictus of destiny, it grabs the soul by the throat, pours anger and guilt on the wound, for a long, long time. Gone. Gone like Albertine. Gone like Karl Rossmann. You don't expect it. All the less as all the more. An apparition suppressed, who knows when. *Verschollen* is the word, none is more strangely fitting for this little paper heart that stops beating, gives no hint of life, no forwarding address, like someone who has died. A devastating absence of existence. Unfindable on my desk, my shelves, in my drawers, in the heap of notebooks, legal pads, jotters, binders. Nothing and no explanation.

I feel as if I've lost my cats all over again, you who've lost a piece of heart will understand, one feels a dull muffled pain. Proust says suffering, ongoing and depressing, is like a graft of coldness on the lungs, unless it's that each mutilation tears my cats away from me all over again, their warmth, our bond

inspiration dead, your only choice is to set to work.

I thought of the coma Champollion fell into when he couldn't put his hands on the notebook with his first three decipherings of the hieroglyphics, at the head of which figured, along with the figure of Ra, the name of Ramses. For five days at least he was numb to the pain and on 8 July I tried to reconstitute a few fragments of the lost notes with the courage of resignation

RECONSTITUTIONS

I didn't want to see the Synagogue—didn't *want* to? I *didn't* see it,

nor did my mother when she finally accepted the city's invitation and went, it never crossed her mind, nor my aunt's, even if the invitation had been sent to them both as Jews-from-Osnabrück, they saw it coming, the inevitable misunderstanding, one of the unavoidable interpretations that lead the well-intentioned historian astray, Eve and Eri were hostages to an honour, a well-meant act of courtesy, for me that's a quid pro quo, my mother said, using one of those strange and tasty words she enjoys tossing into the conversation, in other words: I went to the ends of the earth; as quid pro quos go, that was a small enough payment for an excessively complicated adventure

all the more so as unlike Henri IV who had an interest in getting Paris for a Mass, she had no stake in this city, especially at the price of a religious ceremony.

—We could not refuse, she says

—They'll say Jews are complicated, Eri says

—Don't say that, says my mother-the elder, *philos*ophically you can't turn down an invitation issued by hearts unknown and pure, you must put up and shut up. Don't look a gift horse in the mouth.

—Once upon a time they drove us away, Eri says, then they drive us back, we obey, we obey,

—They didn't drive me away, my mother says, I left in 1928 my bag was already packed.

My mother left and my aunt followed.

—We will go *without* illusions, Eve says, emphasis on 'without'. This she orders her sister: WITHOUT illusions

When I write *without,* thirty-five years after my mother's injunction, it makes me think.

—They think they drove us away, Eve says, them or their parents, that's *their* illusion, but they drove away our families, says my mother, we'll go for the family's sake, we'll tell them: We come for the dead, under our intact names, dozens of names reduced to ash, a hundred at least Eri says, I have seven cousins, I said come with me, first to Paris, then to Oran, only one came, the others, all dead, me I've always managed to escape before I was expelled my mother says, I'm free. —We won't tell them that. —We won't tell them anything at all. We're asking for com- plications. Do your best, no stress, let them bray. How do you say bray in German?

—We didn't attend synagogue, Eri says.—We won't tell them that, Eve says. Besides Baruth the surrogate rabbi was our lodger. Onkel André had hired him. A substitute rabbi.

Substituting for no one, since Osnabrück didn't have a rabbi. Substituting was Baruth's fate. Substituting for God too. I don't remember where he lost his faith, perhaps during the war, in a trench, just when he ought to have clung to it. As God's substitute, his trick was to recite Baudelaire in French during the services. It gave him the look. Was it good or bad, to create the illusion? Since there was no replacement

And that's how my mother and her sister went as substitutes to Osnabrück. —We were substitutes for the dead. And we replaced ourselves, Eve says.

There was a Synagogue without a rabbi. Such a lovely Synagogue! Seeing it you'd think it full of Jews. A young Synagogue built in 1906, in those days Abraham Jonas, the father of Omi my grandmother, the man with the piercing or Persian blue eyes, was the Consistory president. In Borken it was Oskar Löwenstein who'd dreamt of a Synagogue till it ceased to be a mirage and became a grand stone building. In the end every man in the family dreamt of building a synagogue and faith limped, or not, along after them. On the photos it's imposing, with a broad chest and a gaze that followed you. In the end it was a lovely but short-lived synagogue. A brief temple. Length of the illusion: thirty-two years

For me the Synagogue-without-illusion, the Synagogue that moves me and which I comprehend, is the Carcass. The majestic Apparition of the smoking wraith of November 1938. A spectacular ghost like King Hamlet assassinated magnified by the pyre. Before the violent death, one was smaller, more squat. One was elevated by the flames. Here one has the acrid odour of God. And no one left to doubt or to believe. A divine solitude reigns. Nothing to do with the brouhaha of gods and quarter gods and gods and a half that inhabit Walhalla.

This synagogue is a real Synagogue. I recognize it. I can spend hours in front of the sign as in front of *The Slaughtered Ox.* In appearance it's all rawness and bone but if you look carefully at the rib cage, charred naturally, you see the trace of a staircase to the next level, which no longer exists, but as long as you aren't intimidated by visual somersaults you'll find yourself hanging from the very narrow ledge that ran around three sides of the Synagogue, a ledge barely two fingers in breadth according to the women who raised their eyes during prayers, among them the five Gittelsohn misses, daughters of *Kantor*, and Mohel Elias a good friend who felt compassion for Baruth's suffering, and my mother and her sister, who came to the synagogue to bolster the Substitute rabbi's moral, whenever Poor Baruth, my mother said, had to deliver a sermon, a misfortune linked to the fact that Baruth didn't dare tell the cruel truth to the community representatives and especially not to Onkel Andreas Jonas who signed the fateful 1931 contract. He's honest. Was he hoping for a miracle, the kind that happens in books when you pray right until faith starts to stir? But it must have been written that things would end badly once Baruth came aboard. For there is no one to replace Elias Gittelsohn, whose 1931 death came at a bad time, it was the only solution, he's bedded and boarded with the sister of the responsible person, I the undersigned Andreas

Jonas, the widow Rosalie Klein, the community dwindles from year to year, it's not that him that drives them away, only he doesn't know how to keep them, the Synagogue expands, it costs more and more, Baruth loses weight, thins, flattens, turns pale, yellowish, only his moustache stays thick and black, the illusion eats at him, he dreams of running away to Palestine and what do you think he would do in Palestine, his idea is to teach Hebrew, his dream to translate Baudelaire into Hebrew. This is when the storm breaks and everyone thinks it not impossible that the synagogue finishes its days as a barn, unless they find the secret criminal who so angers the elements. A drama.

According to my mother, when Baruth, clutching the railing, ascended to the pulpit, the girls giggled and shivered with anxiety, this, she says, was the death of him. The last time, when my mother came in 1935 and in vain, to fetch Omi, he resembled the shy and gentle animal that lived in place of Kafka in the synagogue. A kind of martyr. A metamorphosis of the species labelled Failed Rabbi. And if Andreas signed Baruth's contract as substitute preacher, it's that under the Wholesale Leather Goods, Onkel André was secretly a failed poet, he used to borrow my mother's French Baudelaire.

Some people tempt fate, says my mother. We know that Felix Nussbaum, with whom he discussed the question of faith, made a portrait of Artur Baruth when they met in Berlin in 1930. Naturally this portrait has vanished. According to Artur, Felix portrayed him with a funnel on his head instead of a kippa. According to my mother, Baruth misplaced this drawing, a charming man but born to lose, beginning with his faith in God, and later speech, and once, in his door-to-door salesman days, all his dry goods, and of course his way to the Synagogue from Nikolaiort, nobody was with him when he died, Omi was in Dresden, I was in Paris,

Although totally fictional, Artur Baruth is recorded in the Osnabrück archives. I find a trace of him in the imposing volume edified like a monument, called *Stationen / Auf /dem Weg / Nach / Auschwitz* by Peter Junk and Martina Sellmeyer, in the section *'Die Opfer'* subtitled *'Zum Gedenken — Eine Personal Dokumentation'*, which is presented as a list of personal data with a file for each *Familie*. Baruth is at the bottom of page 267, without a family. He plays his role. Born (1904, Posen). Died (1936, Osnabrück). Between the two, resides *Wohnung: Nikolaiort 2.* No one remains to remember him.

The Baruth illusion lasted thirty-two years. The age of the Synagogue.

In life, a poor soul, one of the modestly tragic beings.

In literature, he found his place. You find Baruths in Dostoevsky and Chekhov. In the end he unexpectedly became a character of some importance in a play that I was forced, in the interest of truth, to call *The Story No One Will Ever Know*. Right up to the present, and without my being aware of it, the Baruth character is the emblem of the anguished and paradoxical theme: no-one-will-ever-know-his-story. What was he doing, out of the blue, in the court of the Siegfrieds and Gunthers, kings of the North Lands, forerunner or on the contrary sluggard and Johnny-Come-Lately of Jewish wanderings, archivist and colleague of the great Snorri Sturluson, himself poet of the *Edda* and author of all the stories of the *Lives* we will never know? As fated, when he meets his end in 1936 before hearing the end of the Story and so of History, he is killed by mistake and bad luck by his dear friend the poet. As our Baruth died before everyone, and before the War—but already during Nazism's high season— Baruth the character is the first to die before the end, as if he had also missed his turn. Always the curse of the quid pro quo. A character in reality as in a play. It comes to me that Baruth, my mother's Baruth, was and therefore is a character in whose eyes reality is forever a theatre in which all hope and even the idea of a purpose gets lost.

—He had a moustache that I didn't much like, bushy always with a crumb hanging, my mother says. Don't touch your moustache! Omi would say at every meal. When Hitler came, Omi warned him not to try to compete with the fool. He stuck to his guns, the moustache was everything.

But Eve keeps on the shelf above her bed a pretty little bound volume of *Les Fleurs du Mal: Selected Poems* —*Insel Bücherei Nr 119*, given her on 15-2-1934 with a dedication in perfect French, To my dream / To Eve / Who strews / My heart with the dust of stars

—Eve always spoke of it with a kind of anxiety-tinged derision, my daughter says

—He was a failed lover, I say

—A man with no hope of a future, my mother says

—There are many photos of Artur Baruth in the albums from the thirties, I say. He used to send her his ID photos. She kept them. Lots of them in different parts of the album. Framed photographs, with no context, no surroundings, hence no country, no past, no place.

—Who's this? my son asks. This guy who looks like a young Benjamin with the *Dictator's* moustache.

Did my grandmother Omi come to see the Carcass? I never thought to ask. When the question arises, so late, and lands on the paper like a singed dove, I realize that I should have liked for her to have gone there, an irrational, futile idea, or her brother Andreas, or another of us, or someone who might have bent down, picked up a bit of the body, gathered a scrap of bone, there is no more book, but a bit of wood, from a stall, no more tallith, obviously, something living, a stupid idea, childish, pagan, romantic, but which at least for a moment, the moment of this page, allows me to surreptitiously caress the skeleton, for which I feel more than tenderness. No relic. The photo is all that remains.

I often go to see the portrait of the Carcass. Picture a mountain hollowed out by lightning. Picture Hope, that orangutan the villagers chased through the streets of Subulussalam, she was fleeing with her young, weighed down, slowed by her little ones, until she loses one, then the other, under the persecutions, the boycotts, the arrests, the insults, the violence, the beatings, the shots, then another, then in 1938 they put out her eyes and douse her with petrol, photos exist, in her mortally sad face you see two extinguished eyes, the exploded rosace, the stained glass on either side shattered, engraved on the lintel over the cupola's arch the words of Psalm 113 in big Hebrew letters, from the rising of the sun until the going down of the same the Lord's name is to be praised, never had the face of the dying and dead Synagogue so resembled the expression of infinite incomprehension, of spiritual solitude that Hope turns towards the eternally setting sun. Seeing the silence of the two orangutan eyes I wept. The Carcass riddled by seventy-four projectiles. The cadaver's stoning took place as she was still burning. All in the space of a few hours

I wonder who will analyse, and with what tools, the exceptional speed of the execution, the mayor was in a rush and rushed the rushed citizens, the intense but brief joy, like a meteor falling, 'so as not to bother anyone' the Rolandstrasse neighbours thought

The body exposed for a whole day. The photos that immortalize the animal's cadaver don't capture the fear aroused by the speed of the craziness. In reality this could not have happened in a familiar kind of time. It was hell, it was the unliveable writhing of infernal time

Often looking at the portrait of the Carcass I am silent, as before a mummy whose bandages have been removed, I think of her, of her millenary distress, I am sure that there is someone inside the artificial form who still suffers but I don't say so, this is my business, the bones have myriad hidden memories, I am there as a witness, you can't photograph these mute murmurs, but you can be receptive to the messages' pulses.

In reality I didn't go in 2015, I didn't even consider not going I tell my daughter, I don't even know its address, I am on Baruth the rabbi's, the spirit-with-no-synagogue's side. Nonetheless between 1931 and 1936 he stood in for himself and no one drove him away, the faithful, on their side, were perhaps 'assimi-lated' or 'liberalized', you can see them in Felix Nussbaum's painting, the one that resembles a photograph shot through the wide-open synagogue door. Most of the men standing on either side of the centre aisle are wearing shiny top hats they still wore those here in the twenties as in Paris or Berlin. The reformed gentlemen are facing the altar. But Felix and his old friend *Kantor* Elias Gittelsohn, the heroes of this sequence, exit the Synagogue in very large format. Their heads reach to the gallery in which you see you don't see a single woman. And the title of the painting is *The Two Jews Leaving the Synagogue.* In 1926, Eve says, I was already thinking about going to England, on Saturdays *I practised my English with Otto*, in 1928 he goes to New York and me to London, in 1926 Felix Nussbaum painted the gold and scarlet interior against which the painter stands out. Subsequently, after the pyre, he didn't paint the Jewish fian-cée's skeleton. That was something you couldn't represent. Someone photographed the hacked-up Beast, chest agape, rib cage charred, on the right side of the blinded doorway, shoved into a tumulus of rubble, a post brandishes a sign whose stark white stands out against the sooty background streaked with stone and traces of burning, I attempt in vain to decipher the black-on-white inscription, the hand of the photographer shook or smoke has blurred the message. The other edicts suddenly thrown up about the city write hate and *Rache*. I would so like to know the last words to give up the ghost, before the rest of the old palace with its proud proportions. The 1906 builders saw a future as prosperous as that of a leader out of Egypt, Andreas Jonas was not a risk-taking businessman like Moritz and Salomon his South African brothers, the poet's ambition was to honour the city, that had granted hospitality to his father Abraham, for the first time since the ninth century

On that Wednesday 11 April 2018 it didn't cross my mind to go and see a synagogue

by Tuesday the 10th I knew I wanted to see the Rathaus that I could not have seen close up in 1648 or before, or after, before 1881 I could not have set my so-called Jewish foot there but in these years, the 16s of a later century, my foot is allowed, and the so-called Jewish name is written in the visitors' book among the dignitaries, kings ministers businessmen ambassadors, corrupt politicians, shady characters, a whole Shakespearean cast of the noble of heart and the villains and almost no artists. A list of roles. What touches me in the stone stairs and solemn rooms is that they lead to the Peace Treaty, a monument to the force stronger than human hate, to the strange milk of life, to the immortality principle, to the determination of atoms to say yes, to the superhuman urge to start over and mend, to revive the flesh after the bones, what satisfies me is that this monument to the free and independent Omnipotence of the desire to keep life and the force of religions safe, is a modest little box filled with gods and dreams, of inner immensities, outwardly no higher than a prison tower. Millions of nameless people paid with their blood to finance this minuscule chest containing the idea of peace. Inside all is clean and calm and small as the raft modelled on an ark that Vinci imagined, my mother never mentioned it to me, she didn't like History, nothing but wars and massacres, and peace is an illusion, peace is war exhausted, you say peace and it is always a disappointment

—for twenty-five years I was German with no illusions, but already in 1929 I requested French nationality, so much for that, in 1942 no more nationalities, your father wasn't expecting this no surprise for me, we didn't have time to acclimatize, in Osnabrück the Hanover Jews bought the illusion in '81, 1881, it didn't last long, my mother says

my mother never thought exile, she didn't think 'keep', 'regret', never the word 'fatherland', nor persistence nor its contrary, she thought travel, suitcases, not houses, instead of houses memories lots of enduring memories, the only place that stood for roof, root, genealogy, port, in her tumultuous downstream course with its rapids, is The Clinic. A border zone for newborns, thousands of them, still blessedly without names without papers without the fateful official French family record book, at least for a few days, and no courthouse

At the end of her tale she reminded me of a tortoise robbed of its shell.

I read the Book of books about Osnabrück. There are so many of them that I've had to have a bookshelf built since I realized that Osnabrück is a book my mother left for me to read and to write.

Isaiah, in a spirited conversation, says to Montaigne: A book has been offered to someone who knows how to read, and he says: I don't know how to read.—I read, I make some cities my inner books, Rome and Paris live in my soul, Paris I imagine but not Bordeaux, I imagine and I understand Paris, Montaigne says, without grandeur and without place, without stone, without plaster and without wood I find and lose myself there, I am like my dog who barks and wakes up in a dream startled by the arrival of some stranger, the stranger the soul sees, and who is a spirit and imperceptible, without length or breadth, without colour, without being. Sometimes my mind skips a district. My mind also balks at climbing bell towers.

So it is that like Montaigne's Paris, I read Osnabrück, in reality and in my mind. Often I skip a chapter. For example, the Synagogue chapter. One day I found myself in my little car at the foot of a street steep as a cliff with my children and Karin, my authority on dates; and little 'Eve' (my car) sputtered to a stop, impossible to go higher. The Bocksturm is up there, Karin says, the prison inaugurated in 1302 in the days of the Witch

Hunts, during the sixteenth and seventeenth centuries, the tower was also used as a Torture Chamber, today we no longer know which floor was the prison, which the Torture Chamber. If the ground floor, which has no exit, was used as oubliettes, this information has not come down to us, Karin, my guide, in her sparkling French, says. She finds the word *oubliettes* more interesting than the word *Verlies*. Curiosity impels me to tuck my little car under my arm and trudge up. At the top the locked door clearly expects no one. We knock. Astonished head of the porter with her Asian features. Even I don't know why I'm here. The dark little room—is it the prison? or the asylum?—holds a mob of madwomen, in the little room to the right, perched on a high wooden chair, a very tall woman with bushy blonde curls is leaning them towards a fan so they swell like sails, this I think is the director, she's a touch crazy too. And me, I think, if anyone saw my dreams projected on a movie screen they'd know I was off my rocker. Luckily it's not the seventeenth or the twentieth century. Earlier I'd have been locked up, unless like Mama I'd packed my bags in the nick of time.

What I admire about Osnabrück-in-reality is that nothing has changed, today's Warnings are the same as those in the days of prince-bishops and emperors. That informed visitor, my son, notices the total absence of billboards in the twenty-first-century city. This strange mural virginity makes the city truly a work of fiction.

In the Decoration Scene, which takes place in the Great Hall of the Rathaus under the alert eyes of forty-eight sovereigns and their representatives, signatories of the Treaty more high-minded and hopeful than man's first steps on the Moon, in their day the masters of the world, deciders of the life and death of populations, witnesses to the unending series of missed rendezvous with Peace, in the course of which, before the same audience in 2018 as in 1648, nothing changes, now reduced and gilt-framed,

when the Oberburgermeister, an impressive actor in period costume, with the grace and dignity of one of the painted dignitaries, hands me the city medal, that is, the key to the memory and hence to the door of the turbulent and multi-millenary history of this Polis as old as a religion,

the venerable medal thrice clattered to the floor, now the Mayor, now me letting it slide from our grasp, which in a Schiller or Shakespeare play would have been seen as fateful, but this was in reality, we were ordinary, we laughed,

I said that this event, the unintended exemplar of which Derrida speaks, this surprise, this intrusion of disorder in the established and regular course of municipal business, this detour outside tradition but momentary like a dream, this honouring a foreigner visitor with a diploma, which might explain the object's repeated falls,

was the result, it must be emphasized, of a surprising concatenation of chances and accidents, beginning with the strange astrological signs of the dates, the unexpected congruity of my own and the City's genealogies:

in a first period of time, eighty years ago, the City awoke a murderous executioner, a possessed incendiary, the seat of primitive cruelties and impulses, a place of hate and of horde, glorying in its malice

in a second period of time, quite the opposite, the City awakes like the birds, it sings, it is all welcome, hospitality, warm as a crew of Franciscans, it frolics in the streets, the trees bloom, café tables, markets, shops, museums, schools, theatres, the municipality, the political parties extend invitations, the far right does not exist, this therefore is a comedy, a fairy tale, life triumphs, Ferdinand marries Miranda, the Oberburgermeister celebrates homosexual marriages, Mordecai is the sheriff, I don't say all that but I imagine it, I say that this year I can truly love the new Friedensstadt, I came neither too early nor too late, if you could stop the ticking clock of the tale, the time is perfect. It couldn't be more beautiful.

—Go ahead, say it, my mother says.

So I say that no one knows what Osnabrück will be like eighty years from now. My love is precise and focussed.

My mother would not have been able to like it: she was born in 1910. She left just before she detested it. From North Africa she could hold onto its charms, I tell myself walking up Krahnstrasse. Just then the music of the bells pours down on the old roofs, like a shower of youth over the lovely old facades, I see them and I greet them, the ones that enchanted my mother, pealing like the voices of girls wooed by the ardent romantic Germans.

To summarize: everything my mother did, tragedy and comedy commingled, the school and the river, forest outings, she misses the bells and never would there be any others, the pleasure of being a girl, the pleasure of testing the boys, of measuring their worth, weighing their value, dismissing them, the pleasure of dreaming of conquering the world, of being free and not a bureaucrat, of studying the foreign languages of familiar lands, without forgetting without not forgetting, she has no interest in Nazis,

who knows what we'll make of this in 2098 I tell myself in 2018, I would like to know I thought on that April day when I accepted the medal named for Justus Moser, I'd like to know if I can keep it for a while, a little while, or when I've returned it, if I have returned it, on what grave occasion, when without second thoughts I accept this medal that Erich Maria Remarque refused, then finally *agreed to accept,* whereas I accept it only in 2018 whereas in 1963 he finally agreed not to refuse the Justus Moser, but already in 1952 with Omi my grandmother I'd travelled in the opposite direction from Algeria to Germany for the first time, to Cologne, the trick was to not go to Osnabrück where since the 1933 autodafé there's no longer a place for a man-if-this-is-a-man; an honour for him but whose underside is the burning of his body in the form of his book on the

51

Cathedral Square pyre, where his sister Elfriede, after having been decapitated for 'demoralization of the Armed Forces', '*Werhkraftzersetzung*', hence condemned in the tried and true manner of the Osnabrück tribunal for witches (Osnabrück's witches are notorious for their ability to castrate a man remotely using magical thinking), and later resurrected as a street, Elfriede-Scholz-Strasse, is an example of this Reich's extraordinary superstitious frailty, capable of feeling threatened with annihilation by the words of a dressmaker, Remarque writes in his journal, a dressmaker who apparently belongs to no political movement, no social group, no church, merely having opened her own business a year previously, belongs only to common sense, but admits under torture having told a customer, as she unstitched a hem, 'I don't believe he's going to win the war,' reason enough for the Reich, in the hem as in many instances from the Witchhunt Archives preserved in Osnabrück Tower

add to that Elfriede's 4 July 1938 banishment, the extirpation of her person from the Citizen Corps, that is, banishment for life and irreversible, the death sentence on pain of death, an excision which Shakespeare had the foresight to reduce, in the case of Richard II's banishment of Bolingbroke, in order for History to continue unrolling on stage,

thus by myriad vicious offences, violence, still smarting cruelties, the entire city was forever profaned and poisoned for Remarque—take one concrete example: should he walk down Elfriede-Scholz Street, that is walk on his sister's body, with or without her head, or avoid it? —make a speech about the victims of torture metamorphosed into streets or squares? One can't remain silent, one must remain silent nonetheless in 1963 he had not agreed to accept but had ceased refusing to receive, not in Osnabrück but on its territory, in his room, a delegation of eleven citizens, including the Mayor five senators and city councillors a famous Osnabrück radio journalist a photographer two reporters—providing that his rule of mutism be respected and the meeting limited to an exchange of signs: the delegation enters, sets the heavy medal down on the night table, not a word for all words would ring false, and leaves. The author reserves the right to write a tale called *The Treaty of Osnabrück*. According to the terms of this treaty, he will lift his own banishment of the city of Osnabrück. He will die forever banished and faithful to his outlaw fate. In his journal he writes the minute of this event: 'I served them foie gras, smoked salmon and champagne.'

—This is what was running through my mind fifty-five years after Remarque was awarded the Justus Moser medal without which I wouldn't have accepted the illustrious medal with its troubled history, when the Oberburgmeister or me, or both of us let the heavy honorary object fall to the floor underneath the lectern. For the second time, I laughed, it's bewitched I think, it doesn't want, it is rebelling

but two years later when my father was in his turn extirpated, my mother was not surprised, French nationality like German nationality can be withdrawn, she notes the capriciousness of laws and chronologies, she herself studied in Germany as a German in interwar republican Germany, just long enough to get her baccalaureat, then time to tame the French language and stock up on idioms, a sport as exciting as exploring the Oran market with its exotic vegetables, a halt in the Garden of Eden, you might think you have arrived, 'It is I this young woman resplendent under the parasol' my mother thinks about the madly innocent photos on Oran's timeless beach, just enough time to bathe my two-year-old consciousness in gold and smiles, perhaps we are happy, it's Act II of *Romeo and Juliet* and the abolition of the Crémieux decree, I explain to Karin, my German friend and authority on dates, the perfidious effect of the sensational image that fills the front page of the Oran's newspaper, the attraction-fascination effect of the headline that fills a half-page

I see the black letters attack my father like teeth, the paper has a terrible force, you don't know how to read, not yet, you read the movements of your parents' souls, you decipher their emotions, the moods you can't forget, you've seen it all in the silent films, 'it's all over' and 'it's beginning again' Eve's face signals

at that moment, the Erich Maria Remarque moment, the exact same moment, my father falls ill with tuberculosis, this happened in a flash, from one moment to the next like the calamity in the dining room, was it just after receiving the *Journal d'Oran* like blows raining on your face, the *STATUT, of the Jews, Promulgated,* from one *second* to the next, not even, like death's missing second, a gush of blood, without a cry without a word he rushes from the dining room, with a feverish bound, this is how my beloved cat Theia rushed faster than fast under the divan to die hidden there and there to hide her death and I just had time to throw myself flat on the floor and receive her two last breaths. It takes a second. This second is the gateway to the other world. It is the Dreadful Second between the second before and the second after, you turn around and the past is gone.

Eve, his wife, my mother, is left in the dining room, for the first time I see the word 'perplexed' colour her cheeks, her eyes, and my father comes wavering back,

changed

is the cause the mental wound or the eruption, now undeniable, of the illness, or are these two wounds the cause and reflection of each other?

This is not a page, it's an axe, the decree has the look and size of an axe, seeing it thousands are convulsed, their eyes staring, frozen dry drained of their flow of images in a trancelike state that turns those who have seen death to stone, an event beyond the reach of any imagination had circumstances both necessary and fated not designated one Felix Nussbaum, as God an unhappy prophet, to paint the experience of seeing what no one can see without being blinded, you can't see death and not lose your head, in the instant between two instants when you are nothing in nothingness, when you have no more being when you don't exist, optically speaking, a camera still records, in the absence of the subject, the light's final variation this is the eyes' last sigh, stop, and, as after the last sigh, the mouth gapes, literally stunned, the same for the eyes staring in their attempt to make sense of the power cut. To some it is given and commanded to paint the exinstant when the eyes, recoiling from the blow, no longer heeding the mind, remain open, stuck, like the mouth voided of its air

I try to imagine how Nussbaum painted *Angst*, the portrait of himself staring out of the frame after he saw the ghost, it's difficult, in my view he's not painting the landscape, he is painting after a photograph of terror,

Promulgate the word sinks into the brain, it's an instrument that squeezes the brain and makes sensations of grief dribble out, I note the presence of these sorts of verbal instruments, damaging to the brain, in many of Nussbaum's paintings, in the twenty swastika-ed years typographic scenes are as much part of the arsenal as the various toxic gasses, they are fumes of a same toxicity

my father is struck down point blank it is four o'clock in the afternoon and until nightfall he remains stretched out on his bed, his body toppled like a mast, his eyes fixed on the balcony oleander which inexplicably keeps fluttering and splitting in two and warning 'henceforth believe nothing, never trust again,' a long drowning to the very bottom

—not-be-French-any-more means nothing, if you aren't any more it's that you never were, nevertheless the illusion has endured since 1867, longer than the Jonas family's German illusion, my father was on the point of doubting no longer, but the unspeakable part of the pain is the negating of the subject, finding yourself struck from the list of the living, banished from the world, not even exiled, decreed non-existing, is a brutal illness that strikes the brain, grips it with steel paws, crushes it, sets your cheeks on fire, seeds images of despair, paralyses the forces of the imagination, above all convinces the patient that there is no cure

Thrown out degraded insulted accused dragged round the city getting struck and kicked escorted by the enemy who-smiles-at-me, fleeing under the eyes of the curious cast to the bottom of the species, day after day after

Because of the death sentence that destabilizes my father, whom I saw cut down—a terrible climatic fury broke up the family—I can imagine the rage that destroyed Remarque from within, like my father's fateful Tuberculosis, an anger unable to explode in the outside air that bursts the vessels in the throat.

In Oran as in Osnabrück I feel my years full of dead anger stalking the streets, born dead, cut down the instant they leave the house, on the pavement dead birds like indignant cries are hurled in vain into the glassy air.

These shards of cries, they cause the most suffering: the cries of rage cut off in the throat. A vein bursts in my father's lungs

Besides, my father was not a Crémieux Frenchman, I tell Karin, not a Jew who accepts the decree but a Jonas descendant via Gibraltar, *taking* French nationality under the Empire, before the triumph of the other Empire, the German one, by 1867 the North African Jonas was already proudly French whereas the Hanover Jonases could only pass through Osnabrück without stopping, they were banned from sojourning in the cities

—nationality is an illusion, my mother says, a fiction based on people's geographic stupidity, if a city-hall employee asks, tell him your mother was born in France in Strasbourg, don't say I was born in Germany, nobody today knows where Strasbourg was when my father invented his factory there, people know nothing about history nationality is a badly stitched strip of braid, snap-fasteners alone hold it on. I've noticed that once nationality is ripped off it never grows back. After the acts of violence your father never recovered his inner nationality. 'One more blow like that,' he told my mother, 'and that's the end of Doctor Georges Cixous.'

—Once a lady asked me: You're not English? What's your accent where are you from? And I said: I'm a midwife.

I live for people who are no one yet, before the paperwork

I am I believe reasonably calm and not too much of a busy-body

I forgive many inanities. I let them pass

But there are limits

In The Clinic I had a fat cook, that woman, she got on my nerves she fooled me with the steaks

I was fairly clear-sighted but not mean. I wasn't a stickler. I didn't kick her out. Everything was gently done. I'm opposed to trials. There was very little shouting

Already as a girl I must have stashed away a few talents that allowed me to get away with things others don't

Later I wasn't reckless but I wasn't scared

Against the brown shirts I was forearmed

To think that in the 1920s we'd envisaged a cultural revolution one more illusion and the Zionist youth would natter about a socialist country, already in the twenties it was too late, already in 1923 Hitler was in the Beer Hall, the future didn't last long, by my sixteenth birthday it was over, I had my curly hair cropped,

I liked Rosa Luxemburg a lot, nowadays nobody knows who she is, a shame they didn't fix her dislocated hip

I believe I was good-looking, I felt I was ageless

I never had a woman die. I was lucky.

Luck I don't know if it's luck.

Misfortune can also be a kind of luck.

In my husband's day I was not a midwife

I was reasonably intelligent

I was a midwife.

How long have I been in Osnabrück, I asked myself. Tomorrow I shall leave. Tomorrow. My idea is to write the thing that poisons the heart, to look through the cracks of History whence spring my childhood fears and doubts, at two years old, before words, you see everything naked, the faces up above you are trembling. At my age to be two years old is what happens in the eighty-year-old dream, the apartment is a vast crossroads the traffic on edge, I'm in front of the doors they are closed, a president of the Republic goes by in his suspenders, he is sucking on a sweet, he ought to know the cause of this mess, I call him to no avail. I begin to pack my suitcase. All over Europe frantic men and women are packing their suitcases, not only in Algeria. Now look, it's raining. The rain pours down. I look up and the sky is filled with clouds of coal, thick black sheets. I'm wearing my little white sandals from Oran. I'm no longer sure I'll get through the storm. Can you still leave the city? I should have left sooner. And as usual at the border with the next dream, I see that disheartened man who could be a cousin, it's Walter Benjamin the man who can't close his suitcase.

This is my third raid on Osnabrück. When I had never been to Osnabrück in the years when I believed I would end my days without ever going to Osnabrück, I never lacked excuses for my abstention or abstinence. Since I broke my fast quite the opposite: no explanation. I wasn't expecting what has occurred since I ended up going, or coming, a long time ago it seems to me, five years! But what years! Raised and fortified like castles in epics, powerfully built and promised to destruction in this once-upon-a-time so high and so deep has it spun its web in my mind. Just the opposite of Algeria, my other mental country. How did my mother manage her passage from Osnabrück to Oran, it's incomprehensible. Impossible. It was someone else. Eve is a character in a tale by Hoffmann.

In this city of Lower Saxony there are, I'm convinced, under the skin of the houses in the bends of the little streets, chemical charms, a powder, or some salts, something that emits, no denying it, I take the world as my witness, consciously or not, who will gainsay me? But this message, a residue, perhaps, from an abundance of Homeric events, this obsessive incitation like that of the nearby Sirens, doesn't exist in Oran. The secret is geological. The Song of Osnabrück's eighteen adventures exudes the immemorial.

Now, since the Spell of the First-Time was cast, all those who've circled around Book XII of the Odyssey are forewarned, what is at work in this Theatre of memory is an addiction, not unlike the imperative to rummage in the world's entrails with the help of writing, to plunge into the underground mental forests, to probe tombs at the risk of losing your mind. My mother claimed a demon perched on my shoulder. Just as she leaves Osnabrück at the first opportunity right after passing her baccalaureat, I flee Algiers. Later she does nothing to encourage me to go to Osnabrück, a message that for the rest of her days remained unchanged, and no sooner was she on Lethe's other side than I went.

—Is it really necessary to go to Osnabrück? my mother says

Where are we going?

We march down Rolandstrasse, my friend Karin in the lead, it's her city, her history book, she herself is a history book; the book begins in 783 at the crossroads of Krahnstrasse and Bierstrasse, under Charlemagne who, in Osnabrück, is Karl der Grosse, they carry the first stones to Nikolaiort 2 where Helene Jonas *gerboren* Meyer reigned at the start of the twentieth century, in my reveries my great grandmother, discreet but dictatorial, might have entertained Karl der Grosse, in a dream or visitation, after all who'd deny that Omi my grandmother chatted with an emperor, in Rolandstrasse I hurry up and watch my step, so as not to trip on a *Stolperstein,* my heart would ache if I walked, even inadvertently, on the face of an assassinated inhabitant, in those days Roland was going to die or else he was dead, who can I ask whether he came this way following in his uncle's footsteps or if he camped with the bulk of his army in the local mountains, according to me Roland died of anger a vein burst in his lungs, this is when Karin stops, she waits for me to look up instead of walking while trying to picture the Storms over Europe and the human and territorial dislocations ordered by the most famous and military of emperors, how will the historians reconstruct that fifteen hundred years hence, this is something I'd like to read, the metamorphosis of facts into fiction and the potency of the law of the fabrications confounds my brain, me too I believed the Sarrasins crushed the rearguard of the Grand Army and not the Basques,

Jonas family *stolperstein*, in front of the house on Friedrichstrasse, Osnabrück

and which promises me that when I am reborn, if I am reborn, in the year 3068, I will definitely not believe, like whole parts of the world, that the Third Reich was annihilated by the nuclear squadrons of an army made up of Jews and indigenous peoples from the North American Continent.

meanwhile, back in the year 2018, I walk a few metres and I am standing before the wire mesh of tall cage tightly packed with blond stones. On each side of the cage, two clean, well-buffed engraved copper tablets. The metal pages tell the same story twice, of the execution of this unarmed body taken by surprise in the middle of the night in the narrow part of Roland Street, the memorial tablets have duplicates a few metres apart, a magical precaution against forgetting, from one minute to the next one forgets, one is reminded. The soul changes swiftly in the 15 metres that run along the stone cage. The cage is more or less my son's height. My son doesn't read the two times two engraved tablets fixed at eye level for the average passer-by. It is German, meant for Germans. Karin says: *Mahnmal.* Memorial. This was the Old Synagogue. Our municipality wanted to build on this very spot a symbol of the Exclusion. A monument. —It makes you think, I say. —It couldn't be more absolutely non-monumental, my son says. —This is how I was, the Old Synagogue says, when I existed, I was a tall, proud building with white sides, well-illuminated facades, I was a success, but it is so distant, if ever it existed, this past. Once I made people believe, people looked at me fervently, like the cinema when it began, I lived in the most pleasant and richest district of downtown Osnabrück.

A bare space between two houses. Imprisoned in wire mesh a collection of big stones. This is what remains of the Synagogue's bones strewn on the ground after the fire. A neat collection of bones. Like hens, the well-kept ruins in their coop of rubble.

The memorial stones of Osnabrück's old synagogue, burned during the night of 9–10 November 1938

In perfect condition

So this is it, the third synagogue, a calcified chicken coop, or perhaps an expressionist rendering of Niobe's tears? The 1906

monumental—here it is put in its place on this handsome street, or perhaps the big stone tears are Jews reduced to rubble, in the metallic netting not one can escape

—Look at that, my son says, it's something you might see in a garden it's the last word in landscaping, it requires explanation if you don't know what it is

—Well-kept ruins I say. In the thirties to protect the Jews they put them in prison. The prison was in the castle. The dead Synagogue is perfectly maintained. You do your best to be as elegantly reserved as your crème-de-la-crème neighbours. A little farther along Madame von B. takes her car out, exchanges a few words with Karin, Madame von B. is a slim, handsome woman in a hurry to get her daughter to school. An immortal. The von B. family since the twelfth century, in perpetuity. This neighbourhood, the secret room, the Osnabrück treasure chest, I hadn't seen it. I hadn't noticed the parking lot behind the cage, nor the neatly aligned cars on the floor of the big prayer room.

The room, with its gilt column its pair of gilt seven-branched candelabras its velvety red rugs, that smiles out of the 1926 Felix Nussbaum painting can't imagine the fate that awaits it at nightfall.

This is how it was twelve years before it died.

—How young it looks! It's modern. The perspective is amazing, my son says. Compare it with the classical representation of monuments, here there's a different perspective. Compare *The Two Jews* with *Napoleon's Coronation*, the immense train, the grandeur of the Church, the gnat-sized people. Here in Rolandstrasse the people are in the foreground, the two Jews coming out, coming towards us with the Kantor in front, this is Osnabrück Synagogue, the humans in front, behind them, the tiny Torah, the Theba, the priest —is it Baruth? —No, not yet. It's Elias Gittelsohn, this is really not a church. Here two individuals. Where's God? That is the question.

That day, coming out; that is, just in front of the painting, Felix ran into Eve Klein in the street. I don't know if they stopped. If they stopped, I don't know what they said to each other. I don't know whether Eve was with Toni Cantor. I don't know what Eve thought of Felix Nussbaum. She never spoke of him. The first time I brought up Felix's name was in 2010, because of the first big Nussbaum Show. Eve was a hundred years old and Felix was a hundred and four. I said: —Did you know Felix Nussbaum? —They lived very close to us. The parents were unhappy, he was a good painter, he went to live with a goy. — She was Jewish, I say. —One brother went to the US.—You are making Felix Nussbaum up, I say. —I too am an invention. You are inventing me.—Then I showed my mother a picture of the *Interior of Osnabrück Synagogue* painting. —We didn't go, my mother says. Only for Baruth. Poor little synagogue they burned it alive. My grandfather's dream. It was so young it didn't have a rabbi. Instead of rabbi, a substitute-rabbi who didn't have the faith.

—A heap of stones, no sign now of a design. Frankly I don't like this memorial. They show the stones they hide the destruction. Death is absent. There's no ruin. They removed it. What is heart-rending in a ruin, they removed, sterilized, abandoned what makes people like ruins

—*Ich bin ein Ruin / Geht mit Urin,* my mother says, in German it's masculine.

—The ruin exudes, it sweats, you can see nature coming back. The ruin comes back. It's the beginning of a story. Take the *Nibelungen,* the story begins when everything is already consumed. A ruin is inhabited. It expresses, the life lost, the life kept

—Poor ruin, my mother says. It was unlucky

—This memorial is mute, my son says. It lacks a perimeter. A ruin needs lines in order to speak

—It was unlucky, my mother says. Baruth too died at thirty-two

—The shoes on the Danube's edge, fished up and cast in bronze, I was on the verge of tears, my son says. This sack of stones doesn't make me cry

—That's what brings tears to my eyes, I say

—No desire to see the ruins, but everything is so neat and tidy. Clean. The whole city cleaned up, rebuilt, no advertising, exists intact, the strangest of virginities. This is what makes Osnabrück timeless. Osneiric.

—What is beyond doubt, my son says, is that as Karl der Grosse Charlemagne is a terrifying emperor, he embarked upon a violent Christianization of Europe, those who balked at the metamorphosis were to be massacred, but in a different version of the story Charlemagne invents primary schools, later on, under the Third Republic, the French nation is invented, at which time the indigenous Jews of Algeria become French, and right after that they buy Victor Hugo my son says, we are walking up Rolandstrass, the Nikolaiort Jonases have the complete works of Heinrich Heine on their shelves, but to write *Germany* Heine comes to Paris, it's because of love of the fatherland that he spends so many years in Exile, here at Number 9 there was the Jewish Elementary School which the Jews, banned from attending German schools after the decree of 24 April 1933, were banned from attending after the decree of 1938, but my mother never again walked down Rolandstrasse, as for the Fatherland in Exile that in her opinion was a pretty dream from the forties, 1844, long ago when past and future existed still. We walk through naturalized ruins, everything is tidy, well preserved, in an outpouring of old stories, we walk in a book as in a dream, I sense that in a hundred years the books will seem as distant to us as 'the air of liberty' Heine breathed like the heady perfume of promise itself, one of the effects of this unique laboratory of Time is that when you enter very realistic, up-to-date visions assail you, sometimes arriving simultaneously from the most remote of times right to the middle of the twenty-first century, the entire city is conceived as a brief panoptic tour in which one moves in three footsteps and two stairs from memory to memory

—The fatherland, the country, the nation, it's archaic, my mother says, for me it was already remote a hundred years ago, in 1910 when Omi thought she'd arrived it was already the demise of the promised land

This is how the quiet, neat *Mahnmal* of Roland Street, still called for a few decades for better or for worse the Street of the Old Synagogue, before becoming the Street of the Erasure, becomes for me the only true Synagogue. These neat remains, labelled and caged are a portrait of my inner ruins.

Is Eve my Gradiva?

I've been trotting in her footsteps since I learnt to walk. Her feet have always fascinated me. Exemplary. By virtue of her capacity to move from one city neighbourhood to another country with a firm, even step on her confident, loyal feet, solid as oxen. By her sturdy footwear.

It's all in the shoes, I think. My dream was called *A New Posting*. It was a tiny tale like one of Kafka's anxieties. Where was this new post to which I'd been named? My escort, the city chauffeur, gave me the name of the street. I didn't know the street. The new post was beyond the known. Farther. On we drove. And on. The chauffeur stopped. We can't drive any farther. The rest on foot. He pointed out the way: to the right of the dream, that path there. Straight to the iron door. I am in front of the door. I give it a push. Is there someone? No way to know. I start walking. Is this a road? No way to know. I descend, to my surprise, a path rather than a street. If there are houses they are empty. Suddenly, between the dead houses, a view of the sea, a little beach, below. Narrow, none too clean but it is at least an opening. Now I take not a street not a road but some rocks. Brutal bulges as far as the eye can see. Disbelief. This is the way to school? A chaos of whitish rocks the same ivory hue as bones for a kilometre, maybe two. Watch where you put your feet. Luckily I'm wearing flat, snug-fitting lace-up shoes. Supposing I'd come in heels? A fall, guaranteed. And on the horizon, nothing. I continue. Suddenly a crevice through which the sea roars, you might fall, from here you see death. And yet the sky is blue and soft, it's summer, but if it rained? If I hadn't worn, thanks to Eve, these reassuring shoes? I can't believe the students come this way. Nor the teachers. It's improbable. Without the shoes I couldn't have taken ten steps. We're still far from our goal, if it exists. I'm going to turn this job down. I'll write a letter. Describe the thing. It's unacceptable. For the students and the teachers. Without the shoes there'd be deaths. With the shoes a risk, treacherous.

Shoes for every body-to-body encounter with the world's asperities, steep casbahs, night raids in ravines with shanty towns, border and desert crossings. Shoes for each ordeal. Except the day she donned a veil to flee in secret to the airport and had the brainwave of borrowing Kheira's sandals.

In the end, the Algerians, not the Germans, not the French, locked up my mother.

How my mother first armed herself for the daily combat I don't know

PLÖTZLICH—

ALL OF A SUDDEN A PHOTOGRAPH

A gathering of former classmates of Osnabrück High School in Ria Kruse's garden. The photograph was published on 8 June 1985 in the *Osnabrücker Zeitung*. Eve Cixous is seventh from the left; Toni Cantor is fifth from the left.

Plötzlich standen sie vor uns

I look at the photo. It's a phantography, I think, all these women are survivors. They ought to be dead. It is as if all of them had been awarded the Justus Möser medal. They are posing. Eve is about to say: We are greatly honoured to be here by mistake. She doesn't say it. What keeps her from saying it is fear of mis-interpretation. They'll think she said these words by mistake. She fears being the minority: some thoughts are thinking: I hope we are going to get some of those scrumptious whipped-cream tarts. If only you could photograph thoughts! Luckily, thinks Eve, you can't. The city hasn't changed. Bright as a new-minted penny, she thinks. In reality it is another: it was razed to the ground and rebuilt exactly the same. It's easier to reconstitute a city than a moon rocket. My mother is thinking. I feel like I'm walking on the Moon, Osnabrück-on-the-Moon, this is what I will tell my daughter.

Enter: the other team. This is the other side of the photo. Here is the team for the Reply. That is what produces the air of General Astonishment. The Choir, now complete,

Plötzlich standen sie vor uns

is the Choir's theme song.

All these women wear smiles-for-the-occasion. Modest smiles. There's nothing to boast about. 'The Revenants meet up again,' the newspaper says. The feet are what catch my eye.

Plötzlich standen sie vor uns

—'All of a sudden there they are in front of us.' What's that? What's that from? my daughter asks.

—It's an apparition.

—It's a photograph. It appears in the *Osnabrücker Zeitung*, the paper of 8 June 1985.

—Martina Sellmeyer gave it to me. What a sentence!

—It's an exclamation. It's a quotation.

—Who says that? Who thinks that? Who's stupefied?

—'All of a sudden out sprang a black shape.' It's a Flaubertian construction. 'They must have been very attractive when they were young. The mother had all her hair still, with some thinner locks, like bars of snow.' Once they were young girls, they went out together, mocking groups of them, and now we were overcome with emotion like Horatio and Marcellus on the ramparts of Elsinore.

—Suddenly, they were there in front of us, my mother thought, all these respectable white-haired ladies.

—Who's unexpectedly overcome with emotion? my daughter says. Such ambiguity! Who says that, about whom?

—The ambiguity, I say, is the author's, the journalist's. Or Flaubert.

—Who is *sie*? Who is *uns*? Who are we? Who is in the place of whom?

The two camps exchange stares. The returnees are a great surprise for the Osnabrück Revenants' welcome committee. The returnees can't get over the sight of the other camp, the domiciled. They gaze at one another. The looked-at look at the lookers, the lookers are looked at by the looked-at looking on. This is unexpected. The old ladies are struck by a double mirror effect. Suddenly there they are standing in front of us as suddenly as here we are standing in front of you who stand there as we stand in front of you. Each is stunned to see the other, and to see themselves seen. One sees oneself seeing oneself again in this improbable place called Osnabrück.

—Suddenly there they are in front of us! Ria Popp thinks.

Double stupefaction! You are here. To be here? *Dasein.* Alive! Then little by little memory began to emerge from its cage, feeling its way, slowly, shard by shard it returns, it is hard, a slow, double movement, to put such a distant image back together, to fish up a face, reel it back to the shore of the present in order to recognize it, not to save it but to gently push it off again so that piece by piece it is replaced by the new face with which one warily acquaints oneself. The former girls retreat, withdraw, reassume their splendour in the distance, and are effaced before the traits of the old girls, as goddesses fade and the ageing mortals shyly advance. And leafing through the faces of the others, each is thinking: How you have aged! They speak as if to themselves, scraps of torn-up photos pieced together. And you are still alive! Look at you there on the far side of time! Like me, you! Me? —All of a sudden, Flaubert says. And exclamation marks dot the newspaper's wide page as in a scene from *Herodias.* The friendship they were trying to revive was so distant now! Face to face, smiling, they observe one another. The whole scene is an exclamation, it's the mirror effect, it's not just that they hesitate a moment and suddenly see each other again, it's that they see each other, it must be admitted, they are no longer twenty years old. A laugh and the emotion ripples from one to the next and the photographer too begins to laugh, oh! how funny, you were expecting the emotion, and even some more painful feeling, a touch of embarrassment, everything that happened, everything that didn't happen, and, instead of a seemly decency, suddenly they burst out laughing, the Choir has a spontaneously sublime and luminous view of this scene, everyone sees that suddenly everyone feels like laughing,

—it's that we are so changed and yet not at all, thinks one,

—it's that we resemble one another, and, once, thinks Grete—'once', and suddenly a memory races through the mind of Grete K, a minuscule memory, quick and weightless, like one of those tiny spiders, no bigger than the tip of a needle, if it weren't bright red, you'd take it for a dust mote and yet its speed is that of a meteor: once I had to go to the food bank, we were poor my mother was wire-thin, she gave us her bread, 'no bread for Jews, get out,' they sent me away. Then an old lady with Nazi insignia spoke up 'But she has the right' and upon the words 'old lady' the old ladies in both camps laughed,

—you aren't angry? —I'm not angry, the choir chants between the stanzas

'And all of a sudden they were there in front of us! all these venerable white-haired ladies! We introduced ourselves to one another, using our maiden names, I said Eva Klein and the memory began to emerge, the head appeared, the cervix was fully dilated. The greatest astonishment is that of my mother

—And here's Toni Cantor! *Da kommt ja die Toni!* Such belatedness is Toni Cantor all over. Yes, here is the character in whose absence one couldn't get through a tragedy without rotting with hate and resentment, here's the Falstaff side of the Lyzeum am Wall, of how many anecdotes is Toni the star, you can't get along without her, Toni-always-late Toni-huffing-and-puffing, a quantity of comic books are nourished by her misadventures, all of them beginning with 'once upon a time Toni Cantor,' I myself loved the Toni Cantor stories, and now here she is in the flesh, she has positioned herself in the very middle of the Choir for the photograph, that is, for the immortalization, no one will argue with the rightness of her place, no one will deny her the lofty role of secondary principal character and as usual as tradition requires she is bedecked with her famous jewels pins necklaces splashed across her ample breast, and the shoes!

—Did you see Toni's shoes? Thus the refrain for Stanza 3. Did anyone not notice Toni's shoes? Over time Toni Cantor has become a treasure trove for the chronicles

—The shoes, my daughter says, are to die laughing. Like the feet! They've got their feet on the ground, these earthlings. Well planted. Their feet occupy a disproportionate place. For the performance the director will ask ten actresses and ten actors to come in shoes a little too big, not too much. You must hardly notice. —Their feet are huge, all but Eve's, says my daughter. You need feet like that. All women's shoes. Only Eve is in boots. Sorts of sports shoes, white.

All of them wear impossible dresses. Dresses—sacks is more like it, my daughter says. Granny outfits, only Eve is in trousers.

Toni sports a big necklace. The necklace bobs between her breasts.

—*Siehst du!* Eve says. You'd think it was the Oberburgermeister's leash. You see! You still want to be noticed!

Except Eve.

Eve in trousers, backpack, wings folded, waiting to be deployed

I contemplate the photo. It is called: *Mini-Klassentreffen,* 'A little Class Reunion,' in Ria Kruse's garden. In close formation, no space for ghosts. Next they'll head for the Café Leysieffer to sample the tarts that haven't changed

And the Synagogue? the book says. —Who is going to think about the Synagogue, that ruin twenty pages back, *Ne?*

—Now they are all dead, the book says.

—We'll think about that later, I say.

—Another photo. Three women in matching white raincoats arranged on a bench in front of an old white house with black half-timbering. —This shows the two ladies filled with zest for life, who could believe Eve is seventy-five years old here Karin says, this is your mother and your Aunt Eri in 1985, in the middle you see the wife of Peter Junk the archivist who died in 2009, zipping along on his bike, he didn't see the bus, History was lucky to escape, no Peter no archives, one second and it's over, four hundred files in his head, this is a mini-souvenir of your visit in April 2018 to receive the Justus Möser medal from the city of Osnabrück. Today you are looking at it in 2022, they are as young as ever and full of pep,

Eve and Eri mirrored, trench to trench white sports shoes

Eve, her thick hair, her bright face. Tomorrow she will meet Doctor Fred Katzmann. He's not in the photo.

—Now they are all dead, thinks the reader in 2039. A hundred years ago Hitler proclaimed himself emperor of the world. That night the reader slept in Hitler's room all unawares. I write these lines in 2019. Sometimes I'm in 2018 and I believe I'm in 1938

—Why do you write 'he the reader [*le lecteur*]'? the book asks.

So I write: —She the reader [*la lectrice*] slept. Soon she'll go to Leysieffer to sample one of the famous tarts.

First the speech.

Here it is the designated Mayor who speaks, the style expressive, emphasis on the word *bemühen*, giving oneself the pain, first the pain, then, *mit riesiger Freude*, the joy is enormous

After the sounding of the Astonishment theme, the two orchestras of the Choir divide, one half answering the other half on the theme of anguished Humanity, syncopations gasping with humility

The Mayor steps up and says: It's not too-late?

The Late note will now temporize the scene. In German. *Spät*. Always pronounced *Zuspät*. *Viel zu spat*. Much too late. More precisely: '*Kommt die Einladung nicht reichlich spat?*' Has it come / much too-late / the invitation? Has it not come much too-late?

Such is the theme of the Mayor's call and response with Osnabrück's daughters. And the Question that Mayor Hartmut Lause raises with these former-citizens, after having fluttered blindly around the Room-of-the-Peace returns to perch beside the Mayor without bringing any response. Perhaps it is too-late perhaps too-late, the guest reflect, the guests spare a thought for their peers who have died this year, but nobody really is sure of having understood the Question, their eyes stare at their shoes and at the thin crack in the old floor which outlines a pair of lips deprived of sound. But according to some, including my mother and Doctor Fred Katzmann, this non-response says a good deal

Or perhaps the guests will find the response or something to say at the end of their visit, or just before. Or maybe not. Some perhaps have good memories however unfortunate unfortunately, but still asleep, still detained in Brazil or Chile, writes the journalist who is to return at the end of their stay and conclude his report

—You should never say anything when you act the Mayor's part in such a delicate scene, gathering together a group of a dozen persons who have *nothing* in common except this: they have been accused and hunted down in another time and now find themselves on the other side of the scene in the place of the judges and police, facing their ex-accusers who find themselves on the other side in the role of potential accused or responsible parties, it's as if you could never escape one or another court of law, you have nothing in common, it's as if you were subject to the consequences of a nationality you never asked for in the first place, the nationality of plaintiff or complaint.

A person like Doctor Katzmann could think that—an American who would rather have time to make the acquaintance of Eve Cixous—while the Mayor talks and at each sentence the silence of the class in its entirety swells, no one knows how to respond to the Question's trembling. Eri, for example, who is never embarrassed, might say: Too late? But-no But-no. But she senses she will get on somebody's nerves.

—*Einladung:*

Here's the word that paralyses everyone. Invitation! Invitation! Are we guests, then? I have learnt that I am warmly invited to visit my father's thriving business in Eversburg, gourmet foods, poultry, worldwide exports, Cantor products celebrated across Northern Germany. Our Toni ruminates

—And what if we were *to return*? What if we weren't 'revenants', guests—but fellow citizens-for-a-week as in a dream, ghosts of honour, exorcized?

—I don't know where I should put this question, the book says, into whose head? It doesn't seem to have occurred to anyone

—We didn't come in order to come back but to go away again, Eve says and Toni repeats the sentence to the rest.

Before today's Osnabrück, there was another Osnabrück, prosperous, lively, hospitable, divided, with main and secondary roles, a bookshop where Erich Maria Remarque's book sold well, that's the copy my mother has. And before the Osnabrück which after 1881 is European-looking, there was another Osnabrück that devoured its children and burned those of its witches who had escaped drowning.

Eve might have told me that. And in the background of this thought, I could have seen, out the lovely Peace Room window, the noisy cortege taking Anna Schreiber down the very path taken in 1938 when Ilex was hunted down.

—Still there? a reader might exclaim. I too am drawn again into this brief interval between April 1588 when Frau Schreiber, though still alive has, since 1583, has been alreadydead, the day when, informed of her arrest at dawn, she fled before daybreak.

Imprisoned in June 1585 in the district of Iburg, *Wasserprobe* the water test, in January 1588, judgement followed by execution probably at the beginning of April, a woman of nearly seventy, widow of Burgermeister Johann Rotger, who later wed the widow Otto Schreiber residing on Johannisstrasse. Her daughter-in-law too, also named Anna Schreiber, aged forty, arrested, set free, having survived the torture. We don't know if Anna Schreiber the younger was part of Anna Schreiber the elder's funeral cortege of her own free will or following a court order.

From left to right, fifth from the left Toni Lukacs who was a Cantor, beside her Eve Cixous, a Klein in her high school days with Ria K., Grete P., Hedwig A., Edith W., Gertrud S., Thea S., Hildegund M., Karin J. and Anna Schreiber

They have survived, others not. They don't think about it, or only once in a while, by accident. Toni Cantor wonders if they'll have time to go shopping. She has worn her black-and-white heels

In my mother's shoes the secret of her equilibrium. Heavy, with solid bases, weapons, strongboxes.

To the right of the cathedral, Witches Lane, Toni Cantor fears for her high heels, 20 metres, interminable over cobblestones.

If only one could decipher the story of the cobblestones. In the book's mind, Roland Street makes an angle with Witches Lane, the men on one side the women on the other.

Four hundred and fifty witches burned alive or drowned four hundred and twenty Jews deported or killed, five remain.

I see Mama skipping down towards the Hase, with Toni Cantor puffing along behind her like a seal, wait for me! always late, and yet this same Toni Cantor has become the spokeswoman, surprise! the person who speaks for all the others during the solemn visit to Osnabrück in 1985, not Eve nor Eri her sister, none other than Toni Cantor, such is theatre's mischievous art, how to forget such a character, a bicycle instructor teaches Toni to ride a bike after a year the teacher quits, Toni in a lace dress falls into the Cantor duck pond, Toni learns to swim but in a bathtub not in the Hase, Toni Cantor after the luncheon in the City Hall spontaneously declares: 'Today I have not a scrap of hostility. And you?' the journalists notes, 'Osnabrück's former Jews no longer feel any resentment,' the Journal writes. And my mother says nothing.

Toni Cantor has not changed, Toni will never have changed, will never change, in the play she dons all her necklaces before her scene, in her head nothing has changed, as soon as she came onstage huffing like a seal and clinking, all the ladies shouted Here's Toni! it's reassuring, it could be 1925, nothing has happened, nothing has changed, only the white hair, but Eve has changed utterly, she can't say when that happened, maybe all of a sudden maybe not, in Oran? or in Algiers, at the first shock? or at the second attack, according to me she woke overnight in another universe, I no longer knew her, something had changed my mother, she thought differently, inhabited another skin on her eyelids no illusions remained, in my opinion she must have seen to the very bottom of reality as in a distant mirror a hallucination of prison, small-format, like a metaphor of life, a warning.

Memory on the qui-vive, boots firmly laced. And her little agendas in which she notes her wise thoughts and what happens to her, not trusting a single soul, not even herself, never sit down never fall asleep. Ready? On your feet! —Germany? Doesn't interest her. It's like England. Who cares what the Queen does? I told Eri: you *live in* Manchester, your son-in-law has become a lord. It's only a title. You must think that trickles down to us. Jew, lord, I'm not going to tell him I could care less about the Queen. I know how to behave. For the Osnabrück photograph I wore my smile, it's the least you can do, no necklaces required. The Queen has had her share of family upsets, royal education or not, a queen is a woman. I mean, the masses like that sort of thing and one must keep the masses amused. But in America it's not Bush who won. This has been going on long enough. I'm not going to hold it against the Americans, they're the ones who saved us from Hitler and Petain.

—Careful! the book says. You're being anachronistic.

—Who isn't? Viewed from the Moon the times touch. Me I know the undersides of all these stories, all these ambitions, these cruelties, these dishonesties. The poor Queen she isn't very intelligent, she is intelligent enough. I am fairly intelligent, especially don't take yourself for the queen. I'm going to stop here. I'm going to prepare the sauerkraut. Not because it's German. It's the Strasbourg recipe. Look at Toni. You see: the masses want to be lords. The Osnabrück people have the courage to want to be courageous. I'm not going to hold their nationality against them. I am no more French than German. They flayed me of both my skins. I am universal.

—It's like me for Algeria, I thought. I've read on Wikipedia that I had Algerian nationality. Sometimes you have the nationality without being aware of it. Sometimes I don't have French nationality, according to the French government. Since Algeria first arrested my mother, then imprisoned her before, in a later development, being unable to arrest and expel her because she'd given her jailers the slip and, in the period between these two developments, she spun herself some time during which she helped give birth to thousands of Algerians and simultaneously printed up her leitmotifs: *watch out prison, suitcases,* right to the day she donned her wings and fled, while down below the minuscule police force shot their guns at her

since those days the idea of Algerian nationality has fused with the illusion of French nationality and the myth of German nationality.

My mother would not have returned had they not telephoned her from Osnabrück. Except for the German language, that is something she has never renounced and the German language has not renounced my mother's language.

Anna Schreiber also, with this literary name, as she is being dragged beyond this murderous world towards the door of violent death, had nothing left to lose but the language.

I don't know if my mother listened to the mayor's little speech, she didn't mention it, she didn't mention any changes in the city. She didn't tell me about the Jews who weren't from Osnabrück, who weren't Jews who were the replacements, Osnabrück too a replacement for Osnabrück and her as well

I am inventing all that goes on behind the scene of the old girls' photograph among or between those who are subjected, voluntarily, to a process of constant stimulation, each person is at least double, nothing is what it seems, only the Mayor is undivided, enthused as he is, if I believe the newspaper, about the need to touch, to obtain peace with his speech on which you can read the words: *bemuhen*, we've tried so hard, and behind this heartfelt effort by the 1985 citizens is the feverish idea, undesirable, to *abbauen*, bring down the prejudices, destroy them, deactivate them, *ja sie gar nicht entstehen zu lassen*, and even prevent them re-forming, *definitively*. 'They are bending over backwards' my mother tells Eri, in French. —*Was ist* 'bending over backwards?' Eri asks, Eri has a sweet tooth for words in the tongue of their freedom. This is me reporting. If I engage in this fictive but serious rummaging, it's because I'm trying to reach a hidden place at I don't know what level of the reality behind the photo, that explains to me why or how none of these Guests was ever to return to Osnabrück. Everyone was enchanted, and disappointed. There was the illusion, none of them could have foreseen the need to submit to a philosophy test on the theme of my home. Or theirs. Or on them. *Chez*, how do you say that in German? Pas-chez-moi is clear enough. But chez-moi is another affair. Chez-moi is The Clinic, my mother says, that I could say. Whereupon none of the philosophically tested guests can deny that in their mental garden there's a little Osnabrück dirt, and on their fingertips, the feet don't ask questions my mother thinks, 'men cannot forget the soil,' the past is well kept, no way to let it come and replace the present,

My mother's trial, I thought, she couldn't not have thought about it, the confiscations of her being, her attributes, the house, her resemblances to herself, 'Look at the minutes of the trial.' In the phantom tribunal where she listened to the Mayor or maybe not, she could not have said in truth that she was, who she was, my mother above all was in the was-nots, she was not German, she was not French, she was not Jewish, 'I was a mid-wife,' this, she could have said, in this she had her being, in The Clinic no separation of the soul, no simulation, everything is reality incarnate, prehistoric right until

all the Guests go by taxi to the University, where Disappointment awaits. For the discussion, only a handful of students, if that, the journalist reports. The disappointed ones are not the Guests. *Réception* rhymes with *Déception*, my mother says in French.

Johannes Kepler's mother had also been arrested as a witch specialized in deadly maladies of animals, if she thinks 'cow', a cow dies, the trial's records claim, my son says, add to this the boy stillborn to the neighbour the one she'd accused of stealing laundry off the line,

—it's a period of a crazy modernity, the dawn of a scientific revolution cheek by jowl with darkness, barbarism, catastrophes, outbreaks of the plague, my son says, 30 per cent of the population don't have enough Jews to accuse, Jews aren't everywhere, women are everywhere, the incidence of witch hunts increased between the reinvention of alchemy, the detection of the omnipresent Devil and the invention of the microscope, the world is not what one imagines, spermatozoa are discovered, spiritual microscopes find the hand of the devil in people's intentions

Katarina Kepler is on the verge of despair, she denies having attempted to corrupt the judge. The court clerk reports: unfortunately, the prisoner has appeared with the help of her son, Mister Johannes Kepler Mathematician. —'My mother is a cantankerous and disagreeable woman,' the scientist says, 'but she is not a midwife, she detests looking after women and she couldn't be a witch or I'd have severed relations with her,' the Mathematician says. The mother and son are darkness and light. Finally the accused is condemned on 10 September to the *Territio*, the threat of a torture inflicted by psychological means, without physical contact. Taking the prisoner to the place of execution, the executioner threatens her with the most dire tortures, described in detail in the torture chamber. On the morning of 28 September, Katarina Kepler is tortured. The pain inflicted by the specialist's discourse is not inferior to that wrought by the yanking out of fingernails and the cracking of tibias. She remains for a long while in hell, asserting that she is not the cause of epidemics, and how it would serve no purpose were she to admit what is not. At the end of this interminable procedure she is released and condemned to pay the executioner and court costs. The bill is long. To the bill are added the costs of her transportation under guard to keep her from doing harm en route. She must remain in home detention forever. Upon which she soon dies.

—Me too, my mother says, when I was in prison, the judge accused me of attempted corruption.

Montaigne finds that in the case of his neighbours, wretched witches like Kepler's mother with witches' heads, it is better to give them hellebore than hemlock, such is his answer to a letter from the young German mathematician.

What on earth could he have told him?

I would really like to have known the contents of the *Territio*, I say. But it's the *Henker*'s professional secret. The executioner's imagination is differently honed for each victim. One must also contend with chance.

—Look at the court records, the centre for the persecution of witches, those hundreds of women mixed with a handful of men, students mostly, *verhaftet*, arrested, imprisoned in August, then it goes quickly, executed in September, defended by their husbands, disowned by their husbands as in the case of Elfriede Scholtz arrested in October '43 executed in December, denounced by their near and dear, by their customers, their neighbours, their daughters-in-law, condemned on the advice of each new eyewitness who comes to flesh out the procurers' dreams. Two figures in black uniforms represent the envoys of the end. You have a month, sometimes two, to traverse the long-short path towards the last pages of the court record. Well-kept archives. It's like the logbook of The Clinic recorded in my mother's hand. Archives of departures, archives of arrivals.

—And do you know how old they are?

—They are young, my daughter says. Desirable women, worse luck for them.

—They are very old, mostly. Past seventy. Many are eighty. Without the devil's help they could never have reached such a ripe old age

But Eve was a goat, at fifty-two she was a solid, agile midwife who scampered down the ravines of Bouzareah even during curfews

In Osnabrück, women were attached in the following position: big toe joined to index finger. My mother's big toe fascinated me. Big, broad, the opposite of her thin agile body. Body parts hide an edict of destiny: Achilles' tendon, Siegfried's shoulder, Eve's big toe. Do you know Anna Schreiber's story? The midwife. Here's where the cart the councillors used to drag Anne went—in front of the garden—towards the Hase where in ten minutes they will

—no one can account for the overcharged contents of those ten minutes, they are not like minutes, not like time, they howl like dogs, heartbeats gathering speed towards the abyss, a hundred times they repeat the torture, and perhaps a thousand times, you die, you die, you die, water is slow,

you don't know what is most terrifying, the bottomless pit of the river or the gaping mouth of the howling crowd, 'terrifying' is not the word, all yesterday's words are drowned, thirty thousand people invade the place brandishing thousands and thousands of banners struck with swastikas, the whole city hastens to the sacrifice multiplied by thirty thousand, as long as she remains in the cart Anna hopes for the end by the Hase, she has a fiery thirst for the river but when she finds herself on the edge of the Hase, not her moreover but the wheel of human flesh—big toe and index tied together—into which she is changed,

'*Dem Wurf ins Wasser entging fast keine Frauen,*' the city historian concludes his report, 'Almost no women escaped being thrown into the river,' my mother tells me. 'Me, I escaped, I didn't wait. The minute I heard the police was coming, I grabbed my suitcase.'

WELL-KEPT STORIES—PRISONS

I understand now that the Eve's story was already heading for the Hexengang in 1928, a route that in 1962 would lead her to Barberousse prison. History on the alert, on its guard, always ready to take to its heels, and always for the same reasons. Suitcase, House rhyme with Prison, Suitcase, Flight. Her escapes are interesting, they are inspired, something acting the part of God warns her, vigilant as a hare she escapes in the nick of time, once bitten twice shy, with the exception of the Barberousse error—unforeseeable—throughout her life in her thoughts she never stops fleeing, plotting her getaways. Ever since getting out of jail, she remains, ears pricked, house with suitcases right to the eaves, the suitcases are portable houses— your suitcases weigh a ton, I say they aren't any good for travelling —they are moving vans, I see two police officers in front of The Clinic door, clack! I don't wait—, *first* I flee with my backpack, later, I ask Kheira or Monsieur David, to send my suitcases after me, my mother says, fleeing, I'm at the airport, I'll write, a flight absolutely without adieu, in an instant, like a death, like a kidnapping, bing! bang! a flash of lightning, like a sudden awaking, the continent has dropped to the bottom of time

how to stage that? the playwright wonders, an event that doesn't take place?

alone, with a suitcase, sole witness

—What luck I wasn't over there, my mother says. By 1933, I was over there, my mother says. And my uncle was in jail. Everyone, my family, my friends, went to ground. Those who could die before they dug in hastened to do so, Baruth, my friend Artur, that is, was already packing his bags in 1936, he sent me some poetry books and he died, fortunately for him, aged thirty-two, the books made it to Oran in April, I don't recall if it was the day before or the day after my marriage. Over There flutters heavily among my mother's memories. You were over there, I say, or not. I was over there but I wasn't over there. Over There is delineated, a massive silhouette in my mother's imagination, you'd think it was a tower under construction, in the process of petrification, growing thicker and thicker, in the beginning you can still get out at ground level, there's a low narrow door but soon the opening is plugged by great chunks of stone, and suddenly those who are within—those who, head in the clouds, ran right to the third floor in the hopes of viewing a beautiful region's rolling countryside, seeing there was no window no opening save for the arrow slit, just room to insert a weapon— in vain they return to the lower floor, no exit, it's as if they were locked up as in the bore of a cannon

I was abroad my uncle was already over there, already my Borken cousin was in a camp, from there I went to Paris whence I went to Algeria, from Algeria I thought what luck I'm not over there, later, when I was in prison, I hesitated with Here and There, I wondered where I'd be when I said 'in 1962 when I was over there.'

Nonetheless it took prison thirty years to lock my mother up, I tell myself. It tracked the young woman's adventures from chapter to chapter, her fights, her happiness, her grief, her regular ascension towards the light, the crowning of her career, a risky ascension and at the summit this triumph, to be a midwife, a great artist of bringing into the world, in '62, with on the average 250 births a year there must be some thousand or so newborns chirping and cheeping in her notebooks an enchanted folk

I had intuitions of life

men were allowed to stay for the births

not one dead woman in my labour room

I didn't tremble

and that's when Prison all of a sudden arrests Life

The year of Algeria's independence? As far as my mother is concerned that is the year when Over-There turned up on her doorstep

—I don't like History, my mother says, History is Wars, Destruction, Massacres of the living, History is the midwife's opposite.

Nothing is as light of soul as a midwife who doesn't tremble. Every day the creation of the world. No reproaches. That's what makes people jealous. An occupation whose task is to deliver, to set free.

There are also cases of women whom you deliver from an enemy pregnancy, but that's not for the books, it's forbidden to speak of it, they are just waiting for that, the police, a reason to lock you up, *bien faire et se taire*—keep your mouth shut and your head down,

—Enough of these commentaries, my mother says, who cares about all that? The work of a lifetime and you want every detail?

The first evening at Barberousse a poor nineteen-year-old girl was having a miscarriage. I told the boss of the brothel, Have them call a doctor. This is not the sort of thing I get mixed up in. In Barberousse I knew a prostitute who was later ordained.

Later my son will find this ordained prostitute on my mother's list of her life's interesting encounters and occurrences. A fairly exhaustive list and apparently ordained . . . but without any system of classification. More of an inventory drawn up in an emergency, unsorted.—What is an ordained prostitute? my son asks. My mother appends, in parentheses: (*religious order*).

—What sort of list is this?

Twice in prison in a single lifetime is unlikely, once in prison is an adventure in general it's a tragedy, for my mother it is an interlude, like a dream in a Shakespearean comedy, a visit to the desert like the time she went to the Sahara wearing a skirt and carrying a handbag that got broken on the camel, a life among prostitutes that she would never otherwise have had the chance to experience, it went well, midwives and prostitutes have much in common, mainly the danger, the endless trafficking with the moon, the most archaic and vital world of women, at the bottom of it all before the social ladder before the savage wars between woman and woman, in this region that resembles a vast tent an encampment in a well-tended forest where the women all speak the same language, the eternal reservations for the indigenous who sign with all their body parts, there's always one who has a belly ache and two who have too big too heavy breasts, this is tiring, this gives them backaches this makes them laugh, one has a speculum, that's my mother, it was such a part of her daily life that she kept it forever, at ninety she stowed it in one of her shoeboxes, on which she wrote speculum, icepack, short-sleeved polyester lab coat, and it was there in her armoire that I found it, the speculum, among the cartons and the suitcases, when I packed her belongings for the removal, midwife and prostitutes speak the same language, when the madam's eighteen-year-old daughter came to visit her, my mother said give her to me, in The Clinic she'll learn, the speculum is not just a speculum, it's a password to the invisible outside world

the first time it's an adventure, in the long run it becomes a treasure and a key especially when one escapes, what's violent is the entry, the blow to the head, the police at the door, this is upsetting, it's like sexual violence the second time it's the opposite, storms fill the sky, which grows darker and darker, no need to be a prophet to read the signs, it grows dark at noon, or rather day is in a dungeon, twice is destiny

When my mother's uncle after having been in 'protective custody'—*im Schutzhaft*—was released his nerves were shattered but the situation was clear, *Hier ist kein Bleiben,* he wrote Omi, 'This is nowhere to be,' I don't know if my mother recalled her exit from Germany when she exited prison, perhaps not

once is enough my mother thought, I am not like Rosa Luxembourg for whom prison included books, prison is even a few chapters in the book of her life, there are limits, I didn't escape Germany to find myself back in Germany in Algeria I prefer to become an escape artist not a prison specialist, whereupon the second time around she borrows Kheira's veil

The first imprisonment was in 1962, or perhaps already in 1933, or in 1938, according to the main characters; in 1962 for me in my role of supporting character, I was about to begin writing a book, at least I was beginning to be woken up at night by the dream of a book cheeping at my window like the birds at the bars of Rosa Luxemburg's cell; that is, like the singers of liberty itself, and suddenly my mother disappears I hadn't written a line, only experienced a fearful joy at liberty's touch, and suddenly she's no longer there, she's no longer at The Clinic, nobody on the phone, my body's envelope is in France, my brain is in Algeria, all around me a sensation of wall, finally she is found;

that is lost, imprisoned in Barberousse, end of the beginning of the book

—seen from outside it is a solid mass without any opening save for a tiny metal door through which I must pass I feel like I am entering a film of Sing Sing with its tiered stairwells and walkways, it really looks like a prison, from time to time there was chanting, then we were all together in a yard, no French women except for the madam, my mother says, and her orderly, the ordained. And the seventy-year-old cleaning woman who preferred prison to the asylum. A poor woman saved by prison. That the management was benevolent no one could deny. If someone was sentenced to death in a cell, the director couldn't help her. Later I delivered her three daughters' babies. Once they let us out for a stroll on the terrace. The weather was beautiful, the sky was very blue, with a view of the Casbah women were washing their clothes. Your worries, what good thinking about them, better not to think about such things, that way lies madness. There were good sides I loved the belly dances, except for the all-night drumming with pot lids. The worries came when I got out, with the lawyer who was supposed to defend me and defended nothing at all. I don't know where you dug her up. I don't have a good memory of her. I wrote all that down on my Resumé. The Resumé is in the big black suitcase with a yellow lining under the red trousers. The suitcase is in the second closet to the left in the vestibule

That prison of my mother's gave me,

first of all, a huge scare, think of Kepler, I tell my daughter, running around German cities from courthouse to tribunal with his mother on his mind, except that he doesn't love his mother, his battle is of a great purity whereas I, with my love for Eve seething in my chest, I was *beside myself* and all for nothing since I was unable to sit still in France and couldn't go to Algeria, where anyone who came to complain found themselves that very night standing in front of Barberousse's little metal door, on the men's side or the women's side

and secondly, a great and unexpected freedom; I realized, with regard to the book, the dream of the book that kept me up at night, that anything goes—you could recount the silliest. nonsense, extravagate, vanish into tunnels without fear of exaggerating, even disappear in the middle of a sentence and wake one morning inside an obscure building not knowing how you got there, it must have happened inexplicably as in a dream, how to get out, your mistake is to seek a door, but you don't know this is a mistake, something extraordinary happens, I was on page 74, I tell my daughter, and suddenly, no more page 74, no more thread, it doesn't occur to you to think you are locked up *in* the book; until a few minutes ago you thought you were outside with your hands on the reins, the sensation of horror that fills your body is more dreadfully suffocating than what Gregor Samsa feels on the morning of his verminification, this must be the imprisonment in the dark that Edgar Allen Poe so dreads, because he experienced it each time he found himself buried alive in a book, this is not death, it's the descent into the dungeon of the self, you don't need water to experience drowning's torments, all of a sudden, as in the case of Catharina Rüssel *die oben geschwommen hatte,* who swam back up to the surface, who was de-Hased, an impossible, inconceivable, sudden reversal, or like Jonah spit out by the whale, on page 75 I find myself, without rhyme or reason, spit out; well, providing you don't panic or turn furiously against the temptation of a book, eventually you'll find a way out, meanwhile reality is wilder and infinitely more nerve-wracking than fiction, you have to withstand all the torture each book successively inflicts as it takes the turns of its metamorphosis

—Look at this tower, I tell my daughter.

—Is that Montaigne's Tower? In its anatomy?

—Its double. The terrible twin. Its opposite.

They have been there forever. Since the fourteenth century they have the same body. The Bocksturm and its three floors rise from the city walls between Heger Tor and Natruper Tor. Seeing its lovely blonde stone, you might think it held sky, a bookshop, that it is the sober and comfortable coffer of a sovereign soul's most noble and modern voyages, a Moses immobilized, only in appearance, long enough to pen his bibles, a construction comparable to an astronomical observatory destined for a spiritual telescope. What must one do *to see the world?* First, you must tramp around, from pope to king, from mountain to river, from Rome to Paris, Montaigne says, immersed in the world you do not write, you are a retina of black paper the world is printed on the sheet of the retina until the day when you have seen. What remains is to climb back up to the writing, to extract in writing what you have seen. The Vision of the world occupies the bottom of the world, entering the Tower it's on the ground floor to the right of the stairs, the whole room is printed with signs, celestial and other. Here you begin to retrace your footsteps and see what you have seen. In the darkroom with its illustrations I begin by re-flection to see in myself what I've seen outside, the firmament is on the ceiling, my re-flection bounces into the mirror, onto the wall and the starry hangings; at the next stage of the work I climb to the room where my bed awaits me, here my thoughts bubble with my dreams, in the curve of the room at the back the trunk that serves as my external memory sleeps like me, it has the advantage of being able to cross the centuries that come after me, on the third and last floor is the library, the materialization into immortality of the visions, the triumph of indelible impressions, boxes packed with seals and sensibilities. From the peak of Silence, one can say everything

One would however be wrong: if Montaigne's Tower is truly the secret temple of Liberty, the sacred refuge for the seeds of all of science's and all of philosophy's courage, the Bocksturm is founded on the refinements of all the cruelties, right to the most super-inhuman, those, that is, that exceed all the imagination's resources, and are the still-bubbling fruit of long, unending research. Today no one knows which floor held the prison, which floor held the torture chamber. However, since there is no door, no opening at ground level, that must be where the oubliettes were located.

And there is also the Box. A moving box you might say. A cube made of huge blocks of honey-coloured oak, five logs made of wood 40 centimetres thick, the Box measures 2 metres by 2 metres. It occupies a small space, 3 metres by 3 metres, as far as one can tell it is so heavy that it must have been assembled in this room, which it almost completely fills. It has, you notice, two feet some 30 centimetres high set on a block of wood 2 metres long. And on one side a metre off the ground, a 30 by 20 cm-square opening. I examine this Box from the outside. I cannot imagine what it contains. It has a minuscule opening. I stare at it as if I expected it to speak. All I know of its contents is the name of the Count. It is a Box for a Man. It bears a count's name: Count Johann von Hoya. He is not just anyone. The Town Council that condemned him in 1441 bore his rank in mind when they chose the oak for his cell. A spared thief. The Count sat in his wooden box until 1448. If you stay sitting for a few years, the body's muscles weaken, its joints block. I look at the box from outside, I cannot imagine the Count Contained, I try as hard as I can but this is beyond me

    —In those days this was utterly banal, my son says

    —There's only a tiny opening, I say

—The monstrosity of the dungeon save that stone sweats, wood doesn't sweat, you have rats, there's no evacuation. All the prisoners: into wells.

—Eve didn't mention rats. She spoke of happy surprises

In our system too, the idea of punishment is that it endures

In the Middle Ages, they chopped off the thief's hands. Not the Count's. In the end, History says he was alive. History cannot say how often he was dead. It says only what one knows. The box is intact. That's the extraordinary thing: the conservation of the box in a perfect state of cruelty.

Everyone except me has been in prison. Is that why I am fascinated by prisons? Once, the man I love was arrested and locked up, I felt myself violently imprisoned I was locked up outside with just a small opening in the middle that taunted me, since I couldn't utter a peep. Once I was locked away for two days, sequestrated was the word, in the end it was for two days, but without an explanation and without warning so I could think it was for ever and those two days were not two days but forever, in a tiny room with a couple who didn't speak, I don't know why. Then in one corner a man is rolled into a carpet and killed. The person who did that point blank is a bandit, a man who is known moreover in intellectual circles, whose motives I cannot comprehend. Should I be expecting a carpet? I look through the peephole, but see nothing. Imagine being kept here, in prison for the rest of your life, it's awful. What to do? You try to sleep. Perforce to dream. When you dream you are set free but you don't know this. Then you wake up: it's abominable. Suddenly the door opens. Free? Collect your belongings. I spring into action. In a corridor I encounter J.L. the journalist, quickly I tell him what has happened, and that someone has been killed, I toss this at J.L. to warn him but who cares, I run I want out, let me out. Outside: the street, I'm not there. A café, I'm not there. For the moment, I am not. I have one and only one idea: flee this atrocious dream.

That's all the prison I've been able to dream.

SALT IN THE SOUP

To imagine or not to imagine?

—I imagine my mother can hear me thinking, otherwise whom would I ask such a question? I say to my daughter. — And does she answer? my daughter asks.

I think she answers me in her own way. In her own way she sends me her autobiographies, by telepathic mail; for instance, a number of documents float to the surface during the dig through my mother's apartment; she sends me them via an unusual delivery system: in drawers, cardboard boxes, suitcases, files. Difficult to describe. These expeditions might be likened to a treasure hunt, her apartment is a dead letter box. There is no time limit. Suddenly I find or I am found as if by a dream. But what turns up are not dreams, rather sorts of autobiographies, for what else to call these sorts of tales whose forms have no peers, no models, which are the works or brief chronicles of my mother's long lives and many adventures?

In 2013, I found in one of my mother's thirty account books two sheets from a yellowing letter pad 14.8 x 21 cm, held together with two staples, filled recto-verso on three sides with lists of some twenty-four items or elements like the catalogue of a play I could myself have jotted down during my creative preparations, save that recorded by me the entirety would be agitated, chaotic, broadcast like a handful of seeds across the page, whereas in my mother's hand, everything is neatly aligned, each of the 75 articles preceded by a dash, no item runs over its line, the handwriting is upright, firm, the letters bear those infinitesimal dots that remind the entomologist spectator (reader) that their author learnt to write in Germany, even a person foreign to the Life of the Author of this alignment of titles would realize immediately that this is a police story, from the very first lines, no two ways about it, item number four proclaims: *first night at Barberousse Prison,* the next says: *trial,* and so forth, births, abortion, deaths, betrayals

there is no title, though the words '*The Trial*' are self-evident, and without any allusion to Kafka's fiction. On the loose-leaf sheets or perhaps under the pages or in my mother's head, there is tumult, but no thought of her relinquishing the steering wheel, even when the dozens of facts and episodes pick up speed and seem to clamber over one another.

What strikes me like the sun's glare when you exit a cellar, is the alignment, the ranking, the opposite of the eddies and whirlpools that swirl around in my papers as soon as I start writing. How tidy this is, I tell myself. And how admirably economical: in three sheets of paper a volume of Dostoyevsky.

Facts, nothing but the facts. No contemplative states of mind. So, what kind of 'contemplation'? Nothing of the sort that Proust proposes, nor the geologist, nor the botanist.

When I show these loose sheets of paper to my children, I call them '*Well-Kept Tales*'.

To begin, a name: Beauvilliers, a lawyer. This is the one entry not preceded by a dash. A title, you'd say. It might be the title of a nineteenth-century story. But that's not what it is. But, what is crucial, the first line, the name that promises the secret, to name it and this name, this person, very French, who launches the story.

—'Salt in soup!' Goodness! my daughter says. Of the twenty-five threatening-sounding entries she chooses salt-in-soup, what on earth draws her to that?

—That's Eve's handwriting? Gracious! says my son. How lapidary! How dense it is! Dense! Every other line recounts a life. Quite the opposite of a heap of ruins. Stones heaped in a cage is the denial of design. The ensemble built by Eve has an astonishingly precise outline

What is this Rosetta stone?

—Eve's glyphs. What she inscribed to keep Oblivion from devouring the tragedy. And to keep the indiscreet at bay

—What's Lolobrigida? my daughter asks.

—A pet name, I say. It's dated! And I don't divulge the secret.

—There's just one *l*, the reader says.

—It is encrypted, the book says.

Spatially thrifty, Eve organizes her list from tip-top to very bottom. Descends in steps. The principle: as short as possible as tight as possible. One line, one thing, the syntax condensed, thus:

—*don't know the file*

—*woman in hospital not pregnant*

What's this all about?

—*first night in Barberousse (tam-tam)*

—*trial: Maria has no witness*

—*if she is witness-accomplice*

—Maria? Was that her accuser? Was it Beauvilliers? Are they the same? No, no. The glyphs of the Maya resisted for a very long time, my son says. The amazing and true story of their deciphering is excruciatingly slow, we knew that in syllabic writing each syllable was formed of four glyphs, jaguars, monkeys, people, black baby uncertified midwife, with Maria, some murky scenes my daughter says, women not pregnant taken for pregnant women, white mother, pregnant midwife, error: no pregnancy, a good deal of ambiguous paperwork here and there no vowels, the contrary: someone understood that the same syllable could be composed of several different glyphs, baby, my mother says, infant, sex: masculine, error of sex, a purely aesthetic choice, the opposite of polysemy, caesarean avoided, a pocketbook, hidden, stolen, lie detector, unmarried mother (ear)

— 'Unmarried mother (ear),' Oh my God! my son exclaims

— 'Blue baby' my daughter says

— 'Unmarried mother, ear,' is as indefinite as 'deer deer Francis Jammes, fork,' it is the lost sesame, the keys that no

longer turn, the keys the Bible leaves on a shelf so Moses, finding them, will at least know that he was truly at the door to the
Promised Land that night, if only he could have entered, but
these keys are silenced, but all the same, keys, ear fork, it makes
you dream, even if the dream has ebbed away

even if I had to re-cross the river's obscure meanders with
my daughter and son, the three of us, in front of the door's three
loose-leaf sheets, we could swear we've spent the day with my
mother.

No one can persuade me my mother no longer exists, I
think.

— 'Blue baby' my daughter says

— 'Humpback caesarean'

The miracle is not Champollion, it's the Rosetta stone. The
object in all its roughness is incredible

—Why do I glyph you that? my son says. Eve the author,
condenses, strikes, the same element is written two, three, four
times according to the angle, according to a purely Eve-like aesthetic, I feel I see glyphs, in the codedness, several references a
single thing, Maria, no menstrual periods,

—*Salt in Soup!* cries my daughter, I am baffled!

—Such an amazing mystery story! my son says

—It's out of place, like a hair in the soup, my daughter says

—A hair! my son shouts! There! —Where?—There:

black baby white mother, on the right, between—baby
and—*Maria-slave*, just before—*Salt in Soup*,

and indeed infinitesimal colourless microscopic ⁓‿⁓

—almost illegible, a hair of no special colour, engraved, under a piece of sticky tape, that folds over the edge of the sheet of paper and continues on the other side as far as to *wear a veil,* while on the verso the hair begins to creep, a snake reduced to nothing, just above *veil on leaving,*

—Signed and sealed, proof this can only have been written by Eve, my daughter says

—I have trouble seeing what author is capable of this. Dupin maybe

—It's coded. Without being coded. It's transparent. For those in the know. It's for nobody. It's for her. Everything is there, there is nothing there [*rien n'y est*].

A denial [*Nié*]? my daughter says. Imagine if it were to fall into the enemy's hands. The enemy would have to be very gifted. Who is Maria?

—Maria doesn't know how to read, I say. —Do you know? —Who knows then?

—Eve had learnt stenography, the rapid method for taking notes, discreet, a kind of camouflage

—Names revealed, but without bodies, places both precise and imprecise, heavy with imminence, hospital, prison, courthouse, tragedy in a handful of lines a crowd of characters behind the curtain a world with a large coefficient of incertitude, error, confusion, anxiety, flights, veil, lost ring, vanished wallet, a child left hanging, error, sex?

—I'm waiting for the bought child

— 'The Foundling?' That's a story by Kleist, my daughter says

—By Poe, my son says. Not bought, but sealed [*pas acheté mais cacheté*].

—It's like Proust's second notebook, my daughter says

For Maria

<good hot>

<complete loss>

Believer for a superstitious person

—You know? my son says. Who bought? The child? The witness?

An episode that is difficult to recount, obscure, agitated, denunciation, danger, hostages

—I know, I say. There's a link between the entry 'I'm waiting for the bought child' and 'unmarried mother (ear)'

—And yet, my son remarks, there are ten different items

—It works, I say, it's both linear and intertwined

—That's called stenography, you hide a text in an image, a text in a text, a tragedy in a comedy, my son says

—Eve liked cryptography, my daughter says.

—She hated it

—She took messages destined for the general staff from American officers, one colonel was so drunk that when he dictated he would urinate on the leather armchair, afterwards she couldn't reread what she'd written. In 1944. Stenographed in English

—Why was she always losing her keys? She hid everything then she would misplace the keys.

—Here, she wrote *Veil leaving*? It's a police story. A Veil over Oran. Veil over Barberousse. Veil over Osnabrück.

—She left me the keys and the enigmas, I say.

—Why does it have to be a scarab you drop in the eye of the skull?

—I don't know. My daughter says.

—I know, my son says.

—Why did Eve save a hair from her work of erasure?

—Salt in Soup, my daughter says.

—Scarab, my son says. To increase the mystery.

—*Gold Bug*, my mother says. *Bug*, do you know that word?

—Just look at this list, my son says.

I look: there are two columns the same length. Starting with almost sentences. 'Trial: Maria has no witnesses.' Then statements, increasingly elliptical, the base of the column growing thinner and thinner, right down to the base where *Maria-slave* is followed by *salt in soup* as if some secret linked these signs. Or not.

—SaltinSoup, my daughter says, it's to die laughing

'Trial' —'In the Soup,' it goes together. Here we have a troubling, monumental list, with an intruder from the kitchen

—An anxious-making atmosphere, vapours who is it? *who's there?*, there's witchcraft in the air, midnight, it is cold on the castle ramparts

Enter: the Soup.

—For Eve, everything starts and ends with the soup. It delimits a world, on the one hand threats, on the other the soup, my daughter says.

—On the one hand *This side of our Known world*, on the other, the other side, the unknown, behind the metal door, I say.

—Is salt a plus or a minus; does it heighten or spoil? It conceals an image like adding butter to your bread. No doubt about it, my daughter adds, it's a comment on the Barberousse soup. Or else it's the soup served in The Clinic. 'I have to tell Zohra not to put too much salt in the new mothers' soup,' my mother notes. It's inedible.

—Eve, I say, is the person who adds salt to all my thoughts. Does the salt in the soup have the same standing on the page as the delay of *the bought child?* Eve, Eve, my salt

This salt is hallucinatory. In the vicinity of the above-mentioned soup one reads:—*Airport 500 F(ancs). Search.* Underneath: *Eri gold belt.* Gold comes after salt. Salt in belt. Scarab in skull. In my head, today: write, do the laundry. I say.

—Unless the *Salt* stands for gold and soup for Maria: in this case you could read the item quite differently, my son says.

The list's charms are obsessive. I understand Champollion's tenacity. A captive of the enigma.

—The document has turned us into secret agents

Eve-Brecht:

One cast of characters evokes a whole world simmering with intrigue: midwives, pregnant or not, caesareans, avoided or not, cinema-bag-of-waters, prostitute unmarried mother stillborn child five kilos, deliveries seventh-month abortions and, here and there, error, error avoided. And the child? Who bought the child? Who sold the child? Eve-Gorki

Captivated by my mother's Autobiographical List, I must have made an effort to recall 1962, the final convulsion of the struggle with the angel, the death, the crossing of the rivers of time, The Clinic's becoming a Prison, and inversely, the celebration and the warnings—the year of Algeria's independence, at long last those condemned to death are called Algerians, the leaders' fights flare up, the paths of my mother and liberty cross outside the entry-exit to Barberousse Prison, this is the Birth of Algeria, in the stairways she is trailed by a noisy cortege of newborns of all colours and no one who knows for whom these followers will vote twenty pages further on.

—But who is Maria? No clue? Anybody can be called Maria. Even Rilke. Maria, man, woman?

   —It's not—'Midwife (uncertified) wants foist her gigolo on me'? my son says.

   —Oh no, no.

   —Is she Lolobrigida?

   —Oh no, no, I say. Maria is a little hunchback.

   —She's the hunchback-caesarean.

   —Who knows? Do you know everything?

   —Maria is the sole character cited by name in this long cryptic tale, the rest are mere silhouettes of roles, Eve therefore knew Maria well. The Familiar. Like Faust's Familiar. Like Proust's Stranger. Apart from the opening role held by the lawyer Beauvilliers, who orients the reading towards the tribunal and imparts a certain tone to the whole like Bernardo whom the whole world hears when he stops and asks who we are the minute we set foot on the Elsinore ramparts. Lawyer Beauvilliers wants to know all about us and we know nothing about him. Or her. All of us advance under the watchful eye of Judicial Authorities. Now we are being led to the interrogation. This is an exotic version of K.'s Journal, Eve K., in Barberousse.

My mother was astonished to discover that she penned the opening page of *The Trial*, word for word, with a slight difference

(the victim is not J. K., it's Eve Klein, or vice versa).

Look I tell my children. We read:

'Someone must have been telling lies about Josef K. (that is Eve), for without her having done anything wrong he (that is, she) was arrested one fine morning'. Next I say, someone appears every morning and doesn't introduce himself.

—Maria! my son guesses. —This had never happened before I say. Moreover the building couldn't function without her, for she held the keys to the elevator. I continue:

—'At once there was a knock at the door, and a man entered whom she had never before seen in the house. This person was wearing a tight-fitting black suit, with a belt, all sorts of buttons, pockets, I forget whether he had something on his head my mother says. Plus there were two of them. —Who are you? I'd be surprised if I said that. I could see right away who they were. The highest ranking one asked me who I was, if I was the midwife.'

—What is the meaning of this? my mother says.

—It means it was written, I say.

—When did he write that? my mother asks.

—It's incredible, my daughter says. I'm thinking I can see Maria on the heels of the police

—Maria? Maria was her accuser? Maria is the same as Beauvilliers the lawyer. They're the same person?

—Oh no, no, I say.

—Look there, my son points, it says: 'Elevator-*sous*'. Was Maria under the elevator?

—The elevator! The return of the elevator. It worked with coins. With 'sous'! In those days you paid cash.

Sous! It comes back to my daughter suddenly: someone was stealing the elevator money.

—Maria?! my son exclaims.

—Eve never pronounced her name, my daughter swears.

She named it by antonomasia. There was a guardian at the door to the building. The-little-hunchback.

—Maria has to be someone from Spain.

I shall put Maria the accuser in a chapter of her own

she will be a little hunchback poisoned by resentment

How she is going to make a denunciation to the police.

A false one. Paid peanuts by a police inspector.

The inspector's motives

Maria collared by the judge. Takes to her heels in the form of a rat.

Eve K. set free.

Maria pregnant. No idea who the father is.

Maria was Madame Grubach? Was she the hunchback?

—Maria is not German. She is Spanish. She is not Spanish. She is Algerian.

—Maria is not her real name.

—What is her Algerian name?

—Maria, my mother says, we should have called her Spite, Omi would say.

—Just the opposite of Felicity, Madame Aubain's pearl.

Her whole life thirsty for misdeeds, vengeance, jealousy, especially against other women.

—She tries to sell the child. A pretty little girl. She didn't want to keep her. Nor to give her away.

One day I will study the Maria archive.

—A poor unhappy woman, my mother says.

Complicated people. Women who believe they are witches and prefer to attack women who don't believe in witches. Montaigne deciphers them, luminous clarity and generous prudence, in his essay *On the Lame*, one of his very last, as lustrous as his testament.

—Consulted on the case of a miserable old woman well and truly a witch in her ugliness and deformity, I made an enquiry and spoke with her at great length, giving her the best hearing I could

At last and in all good conscience, he prescribed hellebore instead of hemlock.

Certain accused like certain accusers are ugly and have hooked fingers, hooked chin, hooked nose, fangs, the hump, which are the attributes of witches, as in the case of old Katarina Kepler and Maria la Böse, also known as Maria, who had a maleficent name, they are between seventy and eight years old, except Böse, and Meier, who were thirty and forty, but resembled their own grandmothers, which doesn't prevent Maria, twisted, humpbacked and *Böse* from finding themselves pregnant, all this is highly suspicious, some like Anna, the wife of the pharmacist Heinrich Ameldung born in Minden, who came to Osnabrück after the premature death of her first husband, like my mother Eve Klein of Osnabrück, who moved to Algiers after the premature death of my father in 1948, are remarkable women, irreproachable, hard-working, and whose beauty, which is not considered one of the features of a witch, instead of protecting them, works against them, for this absence of deformity is suspect.

Unfortunately, the guardian, who is at the service of the elevator users, particularly the pregnant-or-not-women, and can at will forbid their use of the elevator, is mixed up in the legal investigation through all manner of twists and turns. The policeman's leading questions orient her responses; for example, did or didn't the pharmacist take her daughter to the witches' sabbath? Didn't she see the midwife hold her lover in the shape of an enormous cat on her lap or perhaps even in the delivery room, did women come into the house in the morning with white cocks in a basket and leave in the evening with newborns in the same basket

During the interrogation, Madame Ameldung said to the face of her accuser: You're lying! Whereupon Maria had the nerve to reply: enough of your airs! It's not because you are a midwife or a pharmacist that you are truthful. I'm not afraid of you, my protector is the FLN. Barberousse will show you whose head is lower than their arse

—Do you recall the grounds of the accusations?

—Why the mother of the midwife, an eighty-year-old woman with sharp blue eyes whose gaze followed you every-where, spoke a funny language that wasn't even French? Didn't the accused fall from a step ladder, not long ago, without getting hurt? Whereas her assistant fainted and remained unconscious till the boss woke her?

—I only have tales, my daughter says, the tale of a frame-up, a fake abortion, the inspector's girl friend who was not pregnant but aborted, a bunch of heroicomical anecdotes, Omi bursting out shouting in German: '*du Lügensack*!', Eve struck dumb, the carrots serving as hair-rollers in the Barberousse, the judge who asks the inspector where the witnesses for the wit-ness Maria Böse are, who are the witnesses' accomplices, the inspector who runs his hand over the back of his neck staring with hate at the judge, she was freed by a lawyer for the FLN—it was a woman lawyer I say, Madame Beauvilliers

Why did you remove the silver hooks from your corset when you arrived in prison? And did you send them home? How do you explain that it was Fatma, the cook who stole the steaks, who brought a basket of food to you in Barberousse? A poor mother with two sons in prison and no husband. The woman admitted that after the theft of the ring you didn't denounce her to the police. Why did you keep a delinquent on the payroll? All of this is corrupt

What do you want me to tell you? How to explain the enigma? Why do I buy steaks at the Galeries de France? Why did the new mothers eat steak, but not Omi; and the cook too, although she preferred fish, whereas the old foreign lady with sharp blue eyes eats hamburger meat, we await your explanation. This was in October '62.

Which 62? The 1962 that comes down to us from 1662 which comes down to us from 1462,

and how to explain that Kheira fainted twice and my mother was able to revive her?

It is forever the same archaic play, with the same wretched characters, from Zeami to Shakespeare, women guilty of being innocent and condemned for their innocence, what good is it to be innocent? I was short on imagination, the less guilty you are, the more you are guilty of being innocent the harder it is to defend yourself the more you are overwhelmed by the attack the weaker you are the more irreproachable you are the more suspect you appear, the only person who gave me good advice was the brothel madam. 'Madame K, never admit to anything,' if you confess, like poor Madame Modemann did, that you slept with the devil and sacrificed newborn infants, out of fear of the *Wasserprobe* or for nothing, you are still tortured, beheaded in public and moreover you have sacrificed your innocence for an illusion.

Even the word innocence is toxic, in the mouth of the innocent it becomes dangerous and perfidious, it seems to change virtue into deceit and honesty into a tissue of hypocrisies. In vain the old Madame Modemann bursts with indignation like old Madame Klein, my grandmother Omi. In vain my mother says nothing, the noose tightens around her

—In spite of everything, my daughter says, it is a story with a human dimension, in '62 you can go and see a judge and speak to him. There was also the power of the FLN. The police inspector's FLN got her in that mess. Ben Bella's FLN set her free. The FLN was composed of several supreme powers, the false, the true, it was a still Shakespearean world but recognizably human. A story of madmen and imposters, my mother says, I don't even know who the FLN is. In my opinion Maria was the puppet of the police inspector who ran a protection racket up and down the street—now—Larbi Ben M'hidi, had he known it, I am not sure he would have 'protected' her. Mokrane told me

Larbi Ben M'hidi was one of the just. It is harder to be just in war's aftermath than during the war.

To be completed when the book is set in Algeria and not in Germany. What is missing here: 'The plot' with all its co-conspirators. The false client. The false accusation. The false certificates. Subplots: my mother and the Prison Director. My mother and the lawyer Beauvilliers. The lawyer Beauvilliers and Ahmed Ben Bella. The population of Barberousse. The first steps of the great Algerian people.

I will say

A country in this state of indecision, fluttering between two states,

the state of beginnings, year I of Algeria—like year I of the Roman Empire, like year 9 of the German Empire

the state of ends, the last instants of the French colonial Empire, one hundred and thirty-two years consumed in one, two, three days, or perhaps three hours, an immense people lifted up by two simultaneous, opposing tides, this quivering instant of a whole sea in a second turned upon itself

and all of a sudden my mother, who is at one with the Algerian body as she never was with the German bodies is expelled like a foreign body, like a sea from one wave to the next, excommunicated

when at last in 1971

she departs, in her sturdy German footwear, disguised as Kheira

'arrival' in France, where no one expects her, even H. not there,

and her definition, neither German, nor French, nor repatriated, and, to close,

I'll say:

Certain midwives *verleumdet* in Osnabrück who, initially, fled in the middle of the night, and managed to hide in another city, persuaded by an illusion with very diverse causes or pushed by the demon of perversity, like Defoe's Roxana, like Grete Stalmann who took refuge in Tecklenburg then returned on her own initiative to Osnabrück, then, executed, returned some time later to the scenes of the fatality where the executioner was waiting for them.

Henceforth my mother was to keep Kheira's veil in her Clinic wardrobe, from the autumn of 1962 until the spring of 1971

IN THE SUITCASE

I don't know when, on what date my mother wrote, in haste and in shorthand, her *A Fugitive's Life*, whether in '62 or in '71, or later on, afraid of losing her memory. The document bears witness to her haste and alarm. And the vertigo of repetition. Prison twice? It's unlikely, I tell myself. Nonetheless, the scene is replayed. Once more two policemen. The door. It's a hallucination you think. Two black-dressed officers at Anna Schreiber's door. Was my mother free between her two arrests? Once out of prison, she is still under suspicion. It is a chronic disease of her destiny.

In the story she herself tells, the two events merge. Her escape lasted ten years. As if she'd done a turn in Barberousse in order to escape the Bocksturm with a side trip to Bouzareah and the Casbah from childbirth to childbirth to find herself once again standing in front of the little metal door.

1971 germinates in the belly of 1962. 1962 is encysted in 1971. In its precipitation the story loses its mind, airport precedes prison, the veil comes well after the departure

—error: no pregnancy

—airport search 500 francs

—Eri gold belt

—veiled on departure

—lost ring

the story exercises cunning, errs by mistake, loses its ring, stumbles over Kheira's veil worn not by Kheira but by Eve pretending to be Kheira, it all began again this morning it is the first of April, it is eight a.m., I am Eve at the City Hall to declare the birth of a child s.b. (stillborn) of an undocumented M (Muslim) woman. An employee, Fatiha T., comes looking for me: two police officers at The Clinic. They hand me two official documents, informing me of The Clinic's closure until-further-notice-Inventory. Hand over all accounts. Acting as a midwife in the private sector forbidden. The patients are evacuated to Durando. The staff must request job transfers. Everyone tearful. Eight clinics run by French citizens appear to be targeted.

At the end of the corridor my mother sees the high windowless walls of Barberousse Prison. An airplane takes off so close by that the staff's hair stands on end.

At one o'clock in the afternoon my mother packs two suitcases then a third with her summer clothes. Mokrane helps box up her linens. She calls R., he has a cold. M.D. was on his way to bed. Kheira comes. Gives her the veil. They take the suitcases downstairs.

I've arrived at and left the airport. Adieu Algeria my love. All this in French.

And when she arrives in Paris, H. has just left for Canada. Eve wonders how to say 'The Clinic has been closed until further notice,' in the 'Further Notice' chapter of *Der Prozess*

Suddenly everything is in The Suitcase. It becomes vitally important.

It is the airplane and the house

It is full of voices. It contains the years, memory's headquarters, signs of emotions. A movable life.

In two suitcases thirty years. And the third one.

One cannot leave without, without oneself, without a skin, without the summer bodies and the winter bodies

Sunday 14 October 2018 was crisp and glorious, Eve has celebrated one hundred and eight birthdays, it's time, the last removal, I pack the final suitcases. What to do with the house we must in the end undo? Her body-apartment, inexhaustible: each move we remove, we take away, we clear out, we break a seal and the body delivers another secret

The book of undoing takes years. For five years I have dedicated myself to building an upside-down pyramid

To fit my mother and all her baggage, with its ruins and treasures, to fit Eve's house into my house, to warehouse the wealth of her ruins in my mental suitcase, the job is interminable like the transfer of a life full of lives into the Grande Bibliothèque, that is, the National Suitcase.

I am the Archaeologist of Eve's Earthly Body, I absorb room after room.—Are you sepulchering me? my mother says. From room to room her voice trails after me. Warns me not to throw out her hardcovered little placemats, the ones she uses for breakfast, she is attached to them, I was going to discard them. Nothing escapes her.

When, in 2013, my mother had had enough of this she died, her flat didn't die with her, it guarded the door, waiting for her return, if my mother had a dog it was this apartment that waited, waited at the door

after five years it had to face the fact that she would not be back,

you cannot endure beyond reality's end

The rue Saint-Gothard flat was the body of her body, the only home that she produced, fashioned, made a nest in. It was her apartment the one not stolen from her (like the Algiers one), the one she hadn't fled (like the Osnabrück one), I wanted to install my mother-house in my house and care for it as I had cared for Eve.

I stripped it. Cleaned it out. Gutted it. Months and months. I tidied up, I unfleshed and adored it; everything the entrails revealed I made a note of. I didn't think: I'm stripping my mother. But my body thought only of that.

I admit I am following my own taste for everything written in her hand, rather than for her pots and pans and her little knickknacks

Sublimation and violence: Whenever I'm there I sit down at the cannibal table. I eat a big piece of Mama. In the avenue my mother called Dog-Poopy, that I called Avenue of the Raft of the Medusa in my book, my body shies away, I bite my nails, I have a sore back. In the pyramid everything is skittish, dishes rattle in the kitchen cupboards. The apartment rumbles, groans, let's get this over with, be a donkey, be persistent. Enough! says my mother's voice. I have emptied myself.

Only the Suitcases remain silent.

The Suitcases alone stay alone

High in the hall closets hibernate two enormous Suitcases that must be filled with clothing and rocks.

My son has lifted down a huge black suitcase, the Suitcase slumbers on the kitchen table. I contemplate it: it is dreaming. Where do its dreams happen?

—I am revolted by the forces of order of this little city that I believed honest and left-leaning. I keep discovering no entry signs like dead eyes posted on every street corner. A young mother, raped, with a baby someone got her pregnant with, a poor baby half-crazy half-dying, the head limp, no one looking after it. In vain I hurry to get ready, all my things strewn about, clothing, photograph albums this damn lid that keeps falling in my face. I have to escape. But how? True, Eve must be coming back, but when? Tomorrow? I ask everyone where to find a taxi, nobody answers, little by little everyone melts away, I speak to a passerby in English, his silhouette throws two words in French at me: *Ferme-la.* 'Shut up.' Go away.

Part of an inventory for The Big Suitcase that Eve brought from Algiers when she was expelled in 1971

Someone flings a suggestion at me in a foreign language, I hear a syllable 'Turm,' what does that mean? Tower? or Torment? I daren't venture outside in the absence of more precision. Leave! Leave! But where, without the means, without being accompanied, full of secrets and outrage.

—Incredible! says my daughter. It's talking!

I dare to wake it up. Inside! Oh dozens of gold and silver albums sparkling, a whole life of Eve, costumes of every imaginable colour, yet another whole life. And the Table of Contents: like a sumptuous Prologue to a play by Shakespeare recto-verso in a notebook in which her strong, firm-on-its-legs handwriting presents The Inventory. The Inventory delivers a monologue according to its Laws: in the beginning there is The Suitcase.

—Black Suitcase with a yellow lining

and below:

—orange Dacron winter jacket

— white and mauve reversible coat

—pleated green cotton dress

—beige dress navy-blue trim

—red white blue linen shirt

and so forth, a detailed record, you can't not imagine the secretary Angel compiling her list of all the wild and domestic animals as they board the Ark, suddenly I light up: But it's the Ark! I tell my daughter.

—The black Suitcase with its yellow lining is in The Suitcase. This is Eve's artfulness. The Ark is in the Ark. Art is when the container becomes its contents. My daughter says.

She put the suitcase in the suitcase. She treats the suitcase like a coat, like a book, the way I put all of Osnabrück, including *Osnabrück*, in Osnabrück, I say

—In the whole world Eve is the one who has lost the most, my son says.

—I never lose anything, my mother says

—Eve arranges everything in order not to lose it. Every time there is a threat hanging over her she has departed putting everything in the suitcase, my daughter says

She packed two suitcases, my son says. You know the enigma: there are two locked coffers, each containing the key to the other. That's good for two books. I already have your next three books.

—I've never lost true north, my mother says

—I hear her cries, I rush down, I say. —Lost! Lost! Her hundred years tremble, she is standing up, so very old, without her teeth, panic, four o'clock in the morning, she holds out three quivering sheets of paper: First sheet: I can't / find my backpack. Second sheet: I / don't find / my / backpack. Third sheet: My pink dressing grown / in the black / suitcase / with the yellow lining pls. The writing very faint, the pen no doubt out of ink. I put the dressing gown in the suitcase. I take the backpack out of the suitcase: I grumble: four a.m., terrified. Saved. She says: thank you. The suitcase goes back to sleep. Her eyes look all around for what she has lost, she is thinking hard. Opens the suitcase. A year's worth of memory. She studies the three sheets of paper at length. Hesitates. Puts them in the suitcase. A letter from Osnabrück Town Hall. In the suitcase.

—She never lost her suitcases. My suitcase says. The absolute need for everything to be where it belongs, in its place inside The Suitcase.

—These suitcases are not meant for going on trips, I say.

—Ramparts, my son says.

—You are thinking of me? the Osnabrück rampart says.

—She never left. My daughter says. Not on a trip.

—She always left without going back, my son says.

—Instead of returning, she has the suitcase, I say.

—Each time I leave, I prepare to leave again, my mother says. I have always been up and ready at four in the morning. When I was six, on the first day of school, Omi found me all dressed, with my shoes on, on the bed. Ready for life.

—I am becoming Mama's suitcase, I say, I need to fit it all into a book

—I hope I'm in there? my son asks

—I'd be surprised if you weren't on the list, my daughter says.

—So I am going to put my hat on top of my head, my son says. Everything in its place

My daughter puts the suitcase's table of contents back in the suitcase.

I'm not the one who closes it.

TRANSLATOR'S NOTES

PAGE 7 | 'Here you are no more. You are born no more. You know no more.': In French: *Ici on n'est plus. On naît plus. On est plus. On ne s'est plus. On sait* . . . a play on sounds and meanings I found no English equivalent for.

PAGE 17 | 'absorbed in Alex as the whale absorbed Jonah': Jonas is Eve Cixous's family name; in French, it is also the name of the biblical Jonah.

PAGE 42 | 'the portrait of the Carcass': The Carcass (*la carcasse*) is feminine in French, and is referred to in the French text using the feminine pronoun *elle*. I have used 'she'.

PAGE 44 | 'on Saturdays *I practised my English with Otto*': In English in the original.

PAGE 59 | 'I was a midwife.': In French, a midwife is a *sage femme*, literally a 'wise woman'.

PAGE 77 | 'They must have been very attractive . . . like bars of snow.': From Gustave Flaubert's 'The Legend of St Julian the Hospitaller'.

PAGE 90 | '*Chez*' ('in the house/home of') as in '*chez moi*' ('in my home'), a preposition signifying 'in the interior of', can be applied to a place or to a community, as in *Je ne me sens pas chez moi là*—I don't feel at home there/in that place/country, etc.

PAGE 123 | '*This side of our Known world*': In English in the original.

PAGE 123 | 'It conceals an image like adding butter to your bread': In French, 'mettre du beurre dans les épinards': improve the situation.

PAGE 126 | 'Elevator-*sous*': *Sous* can mean 'under' or 'sous' (money, small change).